BLACKS BEFORE AMERICA

BLACKS BEFORE AMERICA

Mark Hyman

Africa World Press, Inc.

P.O. Box 1892
Trenton, NJ 08607

P.O. Box 48
Asmara, ERITREA

Africa World Press, Inc.

P.O. Box 1892
Trenton, NJ 08607

P.O. Box 48
Asmara, ERITREA

First Printing 1994
Second Printing 1999

Cover Illustrations by Deryl Mackey
Cover and Book Design by Jonathan Gullery
Text Illustrations by Deryl Mackey & Carles J. Juzang

Library of Congress Cataloging-in-Publication Data

Hyman, Mark
Blacks Before America / Mark Hyman
p. cm.
Includes bibliographical references.
ISBN 0-86543-298-8. – 0-86543-299-6 (pbk.)
1. Africa–History–To 1498 2. Blacks–Africa–History.
I. Title.
DT25.H96 1993
960'.1–dc20 93-12392
CIP

Contents

Part II

Part III

Introduction

Blacks Before America had a providential beginning. A client, Bell Telephone Company of Pennsylvania, had requested a book written on Black history. Self-awareness among African Americans was skyrocketing as a result of the Civil Rights Movement. Major universities were being pressed to include curricula on African American Studies. The rapidly evolving history of black people was rich and bountiful.

The author proposed he be commissioned to write a book on the black experience thousands of years before Columbus touched the shores of the New World. Reason? To say to African American children they were *somebody* long before they were brought to America in chains.

Blacks Before America does just that. The story of Clitus Niger is an example. He was a major military assistant to Alexander the Great. Other stories were included such as the great migrations of black people thousands of years ago into Europe, Southern Ireland, Russia, Siberia, Asia, China, Japan, and into Malayan Peninsula, Philippines and Hawaii.

The book tells of Egyptian dynasties and their African pharaohs and queens. The early Christian Church is explored with blacks playing an integral role in North Africa. There were priests, bishops, and popes in the early church. Included is the very important description of the ancient trade and commerce among African traders and the world. The East African ports of Mombasa and Kilwa traded with the world with ships to China, Japan, Arabia and Egypt, thousands of years before Columbus was born — before Europeans dreamed of invading the continent.

One hundred and eighty one years before Columbus was born,

Abubakar II, Malialian emperor sent 2,000 ships into the western hemisphere. Today West African artifacts and parts of West African language are found in Mexico, Central and South America.

Blacks Before America dispels once and for all for black children that their history began in slavery. It tells them that they, indeed, were a part of the first civilization of humans and that they really mattered in all ages of man.

The Homecoming

In August of 1981, the author toured the Nile Valley in Egypt. This was the area from which the first civilization sprang—and black people made it happen. The most impressive and lasting experience was an emotional homecoming among the Nubians. The tears and embraces were deeply moving as he was welcomed as a brother Nubian. What an honor to be called an African!

No words can describe how he felt to be in the physical presence of black people whose forefathers had ruled Egypt.

The dusty villages, the sparse date farms, the skinny goats and the sleepy donkeys tell little of the magnificent past of the Nubians; the museum at Cairo does. Inside is a display of artifacts one city block-long that tells of the grandeur that was Nubia and of their discovery of the science of embalming which was passed on to the Egyptians. The fancy trappings their horses wore during the Punic Wars with Rome recalled how the success of the nimble Nubian riders forced the Romans to create their own cavalry. Then there were iron instruments like tongs, scissors and tiny tweezers and the pottery, clothing and other items used in daily Nubian life. All of this vividly told the history of a people who had both ruled Egypt and been ruled by Egypt.

Then there was the sadness that only the moving finger of history can bring. These people are now the menials of Egypt, the footstools of the economy. They are often the hustlers and beggars from tourists. To survive they speak three languages: Arabic for dealing with the government, English for working for tourists, and their own language which they have spoken for thousands of years. The greatest tragedy is that they are being moved from the homelands they have occupied for thousands of years. The new Aswan Dam is causing their villages to be flooded.

After such a journey, the reading of Nubian history becomes more alive than ever. The author will remember forever the smiles, the pride, the deep knowledge they have of themselves. Without saying it, they express hope for oppressed Africans throughout the world.

PART I

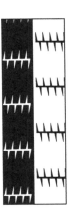

I

The Kingdom of Mali

From the first century after Christ until the Portuguese entered Africa in the 1500s as explorers, traders and enslavers, Black kingdoms grew and prospered in Western Sudan and in the region of the Niger. Their civilizations flourished as magnificently as any in Europe. Their governments showed remarkable political and administrative sophistication, especially with trade and development.

The earliest of kingdoms, Kumbi or Ghana, can record its growth from 300 A.D. however, its actual history goes back thousands of years. A series of economic, military and cultural events saw Ghana conquered and controlled by the Mandingos of Mali.

Mali's territory included the gold mines of the Faleme and the gold center at Takkeda, the main source of gold for Europe. Original trade with the Moroccans to the north was enhanced. Mali rule stretched from the Niger westward, then northward to the Sahara desert and to the south to the Senegal river.

G.H. Bovill in his book, *Caravans of Old Sahara,* says no people earned the title of "empire" more than the Mandingos of Mali. They added to their territory the Valley of the Niger, the Gambia and the Senegal. Mali developed into a seafaring nation, adding new trade routes to the old and dealing with cities north of the Mediterranean.

Mali reached its peak during the reign of ambitious Mansa Musa, 1307 to 1332. Agriculture and the arts were encouraged. The wealth of the kingdom, the splendor of court and administrative behavior were known as well in Europe as in Cairo. Building programs, expertly-governed vast regions of the kingdom and the maintenance of the sharpest armies in the world were identified with Mali.

The ships of Mali are said to have reached the Canary Islands off the northwestern coast of Africa. In 1310 Abubakari II, heading 2000 ships, sailed out the Senegal river to the Atlantic Ocean and to the New World. This was one hundred and eighty-one years before Columbus.

The Mandingos of Mali were the ancestors of fictional Kunta Kinte who, four centuries later, was enslaved and taken to America in chains.

II
Clitus Niger, Aide to Alexander

Clitus Niger was one of several Black men of responsible rank in the army of Philip of Macedon and later Alexander the Great, son of Philip. Clitus Niger, a Black general, was the son of Alexander's nurse, Lanice. He was an aide to his friend Philip and, when the king died, Alexander made Clitus a commander of cavalry. Clitus so distinguished himself he was made king of Bactra (known today as Balkh), a part of the Persian Empire captured in 326 B.C.

Clitus Niger and Alexander developed opposing views on military demeanor. Clitus was Spartan and exacting in his bearing and military duties while Alexander grew lax, despite his excellent generalship.

The Black general saved Alexander's life in the crucial battle of Arbela in Assyria in 331 B.C. Darius of Persia faced them with one million infantry and forty thousand cavalry. Alexander wore his customary golden buckler and white plumes in his crested helmet, mak-

Clitus Niger, Aide to Alexander

ing him easily identified in front line action. Among the rush of Persians to attack Alexander in the close, hand-to-hand fighting were two Persian generals, Ghoesacs and Spithradates.

According to Greek biographer Plutarch, Spithradates rode up, raised himself up on his horse and, with his barbarian battle ax, struck Alexander's helmet with such force that the crest and plumes were knocked off. A second blow would have killed him, since the first blow had touched the topmost hair of his head. While Spithradates was raising his axe for the killing blow, Clitus Niger rushed forward and ran the Persian through with his spear.

In Asia Alexander sank deeper into his lazy, rich lifestyle, much to Clitus' disgust. In a heated argument he told the commander so. The argument became violent. Alexander grabbed a spear and started to hurl it at his Black aide. He was restrained. When the angry Macedonian was released, the conflict flared anew. Before anyone could stop him, he hurled the spear at Clitus and struck him in the heart. Instantly Alexander wept hysterically, bemoaning his act, tearfully dreading to break the news to Lanice, Clitus' mother. She had given the Macedonian army three sons, all killed in battle except Clitus. And he had killed Clitus himself.

III

Terence, Latin Playwright

Prominent Roman citizen Terentius Lucanus was so impressed with his African slave, he gave the youth his name. Thus Publius Terentius Afer, for African, was destined to become one of Rome's greatest Latin stylists and writer of comedies. In addition to giving Terence his name, Lucanus set him free.

Terence became famous for his superb works among contemporary Romans as well as with lovers of comedy who would enjoy his plays centuries later.

He was born in Africa, brought to Rome and sold to Senator Lucanus. His aptitude with figures and letters amazed the Roman. The rest became world literary history.

Terence became a citizen of substantial means. He acquired twenty acres on the famous Appian Way. His other riches were his splendid works, his comedies, which he left for cultural posterity. Cicero, the great orator and the poet Horace were among many who used his works as models for their own creations. Julius Caesar placed Terence's works among the highest.

His works are known mainly for the purity of his language and the exceptionally flawless verse. He is still studied throughout the world twenty-two hundred years later. No other Latin classics have been translated into so many languages or have been reproduced so often. His plays have been studied closely by, and have deeply influenced, French playwright Moliere, British essayist Sir Richard Steele and French poet La Fontaine. There are almost four hundred of his pieces; however, the immortal comedies are *Andria*, *The Mother-in-Law*, *The Self Avenger*, *The Eunuch*, *Phormio and The Butler*.

The exact time and place of Terence's death are in question. It was around 159 B.C. Some believe it was in a shipwreck near Leucadia in Arabia, where he and some of his precious works were lost. A second century B.C. Roman historian described Terence as *fusco*, or very dark.

IV
Zenobia, Queen of the East

Zenobia lived around 250 A.D. and was known by writers of her day as Queen of the East since she finally ruled Palmyra, considered one of the richest of ancient cities. Zenobia was married to Odenathus, King of Palmyra, a staunch supporter of Rome. Zenobia and Odenathus never agreed on the alliance. When he died in 266 A.D., her ambition surfaced and she seized the throne of Palmyra. She compared herself to her lifelong idols Cleopatra and Hatshepsut, both late Egyptian queens.

The new leader of her nation enjoyed battles and could be seen riding horseback and driving a speeding chariot. Occasionally she marched great distances at the head of her infantry.

Her aggressiveness raised the objection of Rome and the special displeasure of Emperor Aurelian. Rome made several attempts to reason with Zenobia, but she was determined to defy Rome and maintain her own empire.

Zenobia met Emperor Aurelian and his army at Emesa. She positioned before him on the field her heavy cavalry, light infantry, and the famous Palmyran archers who had helped Rome conquer Britain. She rode proudly at the head of her cavalry, giving orders, preparing to strike at the Romans. She deployed her units and began a sweeping maneuver which was designed to throw Aurelian off balance.

Roman battle experience prevailed. Aurelian executed a series of pullbacks, keeping his infantry and light cavalry teasingly beyond the reach of Zenobia's armed cavalry and their vigorous forays. When the Palmyrans were exhausted, Aurelian moved swiftly and with tremendous force. Zenobia retreated. But she quickly regrouped and dashed back for a second encounter. This time she saw her losses and fled. She was captured crossing the Euphrates river.

In one of the most spectacular triumphs Rome had ever seen, Zenobia, bound with golden chains, was paraded before thousands of Romans as Emperor Aurelian followed in victory.

Zenobia, Queen of the East

There are conflicting stories about the remainder of Zenobia's life in Roman captivity. Some say she was treated royally and given a comfortable home and that her daughters married Roman nobles. Others say she died from self-starvation, grieving over her lost empire.

Roman writer Trebellius Pollio described Zenobia as dark brown, with eyes of uncommon fire.

V
The Land of Punt

Punt, the third kingdom of the Nile (with Egypt and Ethiopia), was of substantial economic support to Egypt because of her rich trading and extensive and abundant resources. There were "marvels in the land of Punt." This strategic area was frequented by the royal ships of Thutmose I, Thutmose II and his sister Hatshepsut of Egypt fifteen hundred years before Christ.

Punt, which is where present-day Somaliland lies, with the home of the Habashan, who first appeared on the stage of history around 1580 B.C. Along with Cush and Egypt, Punt made valuable contributions to mankind.

Three thousand years later, the Portuguese found the trade routes used by the Egyptians to and from Punt still intact. Existing records show in detail how Egyptian traders and soldiers reached the land of Punt.

The country was said to have contained "all goodly fragrant woods, heaps of myrrh, resin, and fresh myrrh trees, with ebony and pure ivory, with green gold of emu, with cinnamon wood and incense, with apes and monkeys and dogs and skins of the southern panther."

The country was never captured by the Pharaohs, yet 130 slaves were imported from there in a single year, along with gold and cattle. Egyptian treasurer Burded, in the Fifth Dynasty, claims to have found a dwarf in Punt and brought him back to Egypt around 2565 B.C. The dwarf, in reality, was possibly an ancestor of Central African pygmies.

First recorded contact with Punt was around 1565 B.C. when an Egyptian fleet made its way down the Red Sea. The ships returned with ivory and electrum, an alloy of varying proportions of silver and gold.

Punt remained a source of many desirable goods until the advent of Ramses (1292-1225 B.C.).

VI
Saint Augustine

Saint Augustine, the son of an African Christian woman named Monica, had no serious plans in his youth to become a leading contributor to the Christian Church, nor did Christianity hold any special attraction for him. Yet as priest for the Christians at Hippo, a Numidian city of Algiers in North Africa, he assumed his first real responsibility to the church.

His mother had been anxious for him to get an education and he eagerly pursued it. He studied at Carthage for several years. Around 376 A.D. he went to Rome to teach; then in 384 to Milan where his learning qualified him to teach rhetoric, the elements used in literature and public speaking.

It was in Milan that his first major step toward Christianity was taken. His mother's friend, Saint Ambrose, Bishop of Milan, showed admirable strength and invincibility as he defended his own church position against Emperor Valentinian, Roman Emperor of the West, and Emperor Theodosius I, Roman Emperor of the East. More identifiably, Saint Ambrose was an outstanding Latin scholar, emphasized building of more churches, and showed preferential service to the poor. On Easter Sunday, 387 A.D., Saint Augustine was baptized by Saint Ambrose. He was 33 years of age, the same age of Jesus at His death.

Augustine was also influenced by Saint Cyprian, one of the Four Latin Fathers of the Church. His treatises, emphasizing the doctrine of grace, had a personal impact on him.

Shortly after his baptism Saint Augustine visited Hippo, not knowing this would be his home forever. Against his will, he was appointed priest of the Christians. He later became auxiliary bishop. In 397 he became the bishop. Ironically, 33 years from the year of his baptism, he died a violent death when Germanic Vandals under Gaiseric stormed the city.

Saint Augustine's influence on Christianity is believed to be second only to that of Saint Paul. Both Catholics and Protestants look upon him as the founder of theology. Some of his works which are read today by religious and non-religious scholars alike are *On the Trinity*, *City of God*, *Confessions* and *On the Works of Monks*.

Scores of Black schools, colleges, and religious institutions in America are named after Saint Augustine.

VII
Egypt's Twenty-Fifth Black Dynasty

In the eighth century before Christ, the Black Cushite kings moved to challenge the throne of mighty Egypt, commander of their money, tribute, grain and military services. Kashta, the Libyan king, launched the war. He conquered the country as far as Thebes, the capital of Upper Egypt.

Piankhy, Kashta's son and King of Nubia, was made supreme commander of all the Black armies. He completed the conquest. He personally accepted the surrender of Osorkon II and priceless treasures in tribute. Piankhy became Pharaoh of Egypt and King of Cush. His territory extended from the borders of Ethiopia to the Mediterranean.

Next came Shabaka, who practiced double diplomacy with the ever-threatening King Sargon II and his Assyrian forces from Asia Minor. He lost a key battle with the king's nephew, Esarhaddon, who captured Memphis. However, it was Shabaka who actually reunited Egypt and made official for history the Twenty-Fifth Dynasty of Black African Pharaohs. He solved the annoyance from the Assyrians by sending Taharka, a skilled young soldier and son of Piankhy, after the enemy. Taharka destroyed the Assyrian garrisons. He headquartered at Tanis where he could watch the persistent, growing Assyrian menace. They had already colonized Palestine.

Taharka is the same *Tirharka* in the Bible, the Black general who led an Ethiopian army in support of Israelite Hezikiah against Assyrian King Sennacherib.

Later Taharka had to flee Egypt before the invading Assyrian army of Ashurbanipal, son of Esarhaddon. Yet the Black support of Upper Egypt was maintained and there was a chance to recover. Taharka's nephew, Tanutamon, was next in line. Immediately he warred against the Assyrians and also the Egyptians. The latter had thrown their loyalties to the Asians. Tanutamon recaptured Memphis and restored Black rule to Northern Egypt.

The Twenty Fifth Dynasty came to an end around 656 B.C. when decisive Assyrian victories made Necho, an Asian, governor-general of the nation.

In addition to the military accomplishments which held Egypt together, the Black kings of the Twenty-Fifth Dynasty did much to restore much of Egypt's culture and previous splendor.

VIII
The Smelting of Iron

Nothing changed the political, military and economic (farming especially) aspects of the ancient world more than the discovery of iron and the skills acquired for smelting it. Dr. Charles Wesley and Dr. Carter G. Woodson, in their book *The Story of the Negro Retold*, point to the Lake region of West Africa where men first learned the use of iron. Africans became the most efficient of all metal workers which resulted in more overland trade across the Sahara to the Mediterranean markets.

Some scientists researching in northern Nigeria found evidences of iron working during the time of Christ. Iron ore was, and still is, plentiful in parts of West Africa.

Some of the political changes iron brought were through superior weaponry. In ancient times iron became the ultimate weapon, replacing ivory, bronze and hard wood. The ancient Kingdom of Ghana, the early state which was the stepping stone for greater Mali and even great Songhay, used iron to unite its smaller states-neighbors with the use of iron spears and lances.

World known German-American anthropologist Franz Boaz believed the iron was indeed first smelted and used in West Africa, in the same area just mentioned.

Basil Davidson in his *Lost Cities of Africa* differs, in part, with the origin of iron smelting and ultimate weaponry; he says that by 1300 B.C. it was used effectively by the Hittites, then the aggressive Assyrians. The latter, he claims, won battles over Israel and Egypt, down to the capture of Thebes which ended the Kushite (Black) rule of Egypt. Davidson seems to feel Kush suffered unnecessarily because there was an abundance of iron at hand and there were trees to provide the charcoal to smelt it. However, two centuries before Christ, Kush engaged in the trade seriously and smelting became an enormous activity. Researchers have found huge piles of slag and the furnaces in which the iron was smelted and fashioned into tools and weapons. It was ancient Meroe which became the most productive center for iron smelting.

By 1200 A.D. Ethiopia was producing the best swords, spears, kitchenware and farming tools. It was Basil Davidson who said this needed discovery and great demand for iron by the rest of the world caused the doors of Africa to be battered down.

When the Portuguese reached the mouth of the Congo eighteen hundred years later, they found evidence of blacksmiths having been organized into an ironworking elite society which included kings and princes.

African slaves brought to America have left great beauty of their ironworking skills, as seen in Charleston, Savannah and New Orleans.

IX
Blacks: Centuries of Christianity

When official Christianity was only four hundred years old and its existence was turbulent and violent, Abraha, Emperor of Ethiopia, declared Christianity to be the religion of his country. He built temples, allowed churches to be erected, and opened the doors forever for troubled Christians from hostile lands. With both words and military force, Abraha took the Christian message to Yemen, throughout Arabia and to Mecca. Ironically, had he not acclaimed Christianity, the white European Christians might never have gained a foothold in Africa. As of this date, Christianity has lived continuously in Ethiopia longer than in any other nation of the world.

The real thrust of early Portuguese traders and developers into Africa, along with their missionaries, was to destroy Arab power and to break the Islamic control of overland key trade routes to the East. However, the expressed theory was to combine African and European Christians against the Arabs. When the baptized king of the Congo saw the ultimate reason for the technical assistance to his country, the tradesmen and the missionaries, it was too late. Slavery and exploitation had come with Christianity.

On American and European slavery and Christianity, both vital parts of the Black man's life for almost seven hundred years, W. E. Du Bois had this to say:

> Admittedly African slavery was thousands of years old, and was bad at its best. But it took Christians to turn it into a thing of total degeneracy whose single purpose was to reduce men of different color and background to animals; animals with hands to provide profit and pleasure for their master.

As for participation in the growth and development of Christianity, history writer and prolific researcher J.A. Rogers points to *Liber Pontificalis*, the Book of Popes, translated by L.R. Loomis in 1916. He claims there were three African Popes in the Catholic Church. They were Victor, 189 to 199 A.D., Melchiades, or Miltiades, 311, and Gelasius, 496. He contends it was Melchiades who led Christianity to final triumph against the Roman Empire. All three Popes came from the same region of Africa which was, and still is, predominantly Black.

There are other Black Catholic fathers of the church. Saint Augustine was the Bishop of Hippo and the founder of theology. Tertullian, a Carthaginian, made Latin the language of the church. Cyprian, also a Carthaginian, was one of the Four Latin Fathers of the Church.

Because of his tireless work as an apprentice surgeon, then a physician, the founder of the first orphanage in Peru, Martin de Porres, was made a member of the Dominican Order in 1639. Two centuries after his death, Pope Gregory gave him the title "Blessed." In 1962 Martin de Porres became the first Black saint in the Western hemisphere.

X

Black Africans and Gold

Until the discovery of gold in the New World by Spanish explorers, Black Africa has been the main source of the world's supply. Gold had been the economic mainstay of African countries, states and kingdoms. It was their bargaining piece, their strength and their prestige. Whether they were the original discoverers of gold or not, records do show they were mining the precious metal 4000 years before Christ. They traded it with ancient Egypt and Arabia. In 2700 B.C. they were making jewelry and other artifacts from gold.

Around 1000 B.C. King Solomon of Judah had wanted to meet

the famous Ethiopian trader Tamrin from whom the king wanted to buy some of "the red gold of Ethiopia." This accomplished, Tamrin returned to Sheba and told Makeda, the Queen of Sheba, of the wonders of Solomon's kingdom. She was overcome with interest, and the rest is reported in the Bible (I Kings, 10:10). The Queen journeyed to Judah and presented Solomon with 120 talents of gold. This amounted to $3,690,000.

Without question, from antiquity throughout the periods of African kingdoms from 300 A.D. through the Middle Ages, including the sixteenth century, all evidence points to Black Africans as the major suppliers of gold and to her goldsmiths as the greatest artisans.

The valuable skills of African goldsmiths came down from one generation to another for thousands of years. Eighth Century Ghana was called "the land of gold" by Arab writer El Fazari. The Sonike Ghanians went to Sijilnasa to exchange gold for salt. The miners at Wangara needed salt so badly, they exchanged equal weights of gold for salt. Mines of the Faleme and Banbuk operated profitable exchanges with the Moroccan caravans from Raflait and Dara. Later, around 950 A.D., Arab traveler Masudi said, "The kingdom of Ghana is of great importance and it adjoins the land of the gold mines."

The world was amazed by the tremendous amounts of gold taken on pilgrimages to Mecca by two emperors. Mansa Musa took three hundred camels laden with three hundred pounds of gold each. Askia the Great of Songhay, taking the same 6000-mile journey, gave 300,000 pieces of gold to Mecca, Medina and other holy cities.

Despite the extensive farming and vast amounts of cattle raised, history remembers Africa, both ancient and medieval, as being the source of the precious metal.

XI
The University at Sankore

In addition to encouraging production at his copper mines in part of his empire, and his developing trade with Tunis and Egypt, Mansa Musa encouraged learning. It was his Koramic scholars who lay the foundation for the full university at Sankore, the university which brought learning to West Africa and the Near East.

Sonni Ali, who became King of Songhay, founded the dynasty which eventually replaced Mali as the great power in the Western Sudan. In the 15th century Songhay grew even larger, and the University of Sankore prevailed and grew. It attracted thousands of students from all over West Africa and foreign countries as well. African and Arab scholars taught literature, law, medicine and geography, science and art. Art included engineering and building trades. There were exchange programs and exchange student programs with universities in Spain.

There were parts of the university system at Jenne, Gao, Walata and Timbuctu. In the latter, trade and learning were deeply rooted. There was a basic difference between two major cities and their respective branches of the university.

Most of the scholars at Jenne were Africans. Those at Timbuctu were of Berber descent.

Admission requirements to the University at Sankore were strict and exacting. But thousands of young West African men crowded into its classrooms. All came for the training needed for them to return to their areas and to service.

XII
Imhotep, Black Egyptian Physician

Imhotep, physician to King Zoser of Egypt, was also prime minister during the Third Egyptian Dynasty in 2780 B.C. His medical practice included physical and mental cases. He practiced two thousand years before the birth of Hippocrates, who the Greeks called the father of medicine. Imhotep's medical knowledge was copied by the Greeks and then the Romans. According to Sir William Osler, famous Canadian physician and historian, in his book *A Concise History of Medicine*, he was "The first figure of a physician to stand out clearly from the mist of antiquity."

His versatility was much like that of the later Leonardo da Vinci. Imhotep was a scribe, sage, architect, astronomer, collector, priest, and magician. In ancient Egypt, as in parts of today's Africa, medicine and magic were logical allies. As poet and philosopher some of Imhotep's messages have been handed down to the present. One of his long remembered expressions is,"Eat, drink and be merry for tomorrow we shall die."

In his medical surroundings, Imhotep treated diseases of the bone, stomach, abdomen, rectum, bladder and eyes. He detected ailments by the shape, condition and color of visible parts of the body such as the tongue, hair, nails and skin. He treated decayed teeth and decayed bone of the mouth, gallstones, tuberculosis, gout, appendicitis, mastoid diseases, and rheumatoid arthritis. He and his contemporaries practiced surgery, extracted medicines from plants and, like today's doctors, listened to sounds from the body's organs such as heart, lungs, and stomach. He knew the positions and the functions of vital organs of the body and about the circulation of the blood.

As a builder and architect, he supervised the building of the Stepped Pyramids.

Ethiopian portraits show Imhotep as Black. French writer Gerald Massey describes him a Black. After his death, Imhotep's fame increased from medical demigod between 2850 B.C. and 525 B.C., then to full deity until 550 A.D.

At Philae, an island on the Nile river above the Aswan dam, there is a temple built in his honor. A moving inscription to him reads:

> Chancellor of the King of Lower Egypt, Chief Under The King of Upper Egypt, Administrator of the Great Mansion, Hereditary Noble, Heliopolitan High Priest...Imhotep.

XIII

The Falashas, The Black Jews

Today there are thousands of Blacks in Ethiopia, India, Egypt and Israel who claim to be the original Jews; the chosen people. Facing constant ideological conflict with the *white* Jews, the Falashas, the Black Jews, say they are the direct lineal family of Abraham, the first Jew. Funk and Wagnalls' *The Jewish Encyclopedia* describes the Falashas extensively.

In 947 A.D. the Falashas, under the leadership of Queen Judith, forced from the Ethiopian throne the ruling line of Solomon and Sheba. The Falashas ruled the nation for 40 years. The late Haile Selassie, self-pronounced Lion of Judah and King of Kings, was the last of the Solomon-Sheba line. He was forced from the throne and died in house arrest in 1979. He mounted the throne in 1930.

M. Fishberg, in his book *North African Jews* (New York, 1910), says of the Falashas, "They are of the Negro type. The fuzzy hair... and other identifiable factors." H. Norden in "Among the Black

Jews" from his book *Africa's Last Empire*, says "They became (to me) the records of life of a people not unlike the Falashas."

Rudolph R. Windson's detailed book, *From Babylon To Timbuctu* (New York, 1969), supports the position of the Falashas to his point: he says Terah, Abraham's father, came from the land of Ur of the Chaldees which was located in the southern part of the Euphrates. The Chaldees were one of many Cushite tribes and Cushite means Black according to the Bible dictionary. Windsor goes on by saying, "Cush, a son of Ham, and his descendants, appeared to have spread along tracts extending from the higher Nile to the Euphrates and Tigris rivers."

History affords many connections between Babylon, Arabia and Ethiopia. "There is more than adequate evidence," Windsor continues, "that the ancient nations of Babylon, Sumer, Akkadia and the Chaldea were inhabited by Cushite tribes on all sides of the Tigris and Euphrates rivers."

The Ethiopia of today descended from the Auximite Empire dating back to 1800 years before Christ. The remaining Solomon and Sheba line lists kings from Ori in 478 B.C. to Selassie in 1930.

H.Norden says of the Abyssinian Jews, or the Falashas, "My stay among them carried something of the quality of interest and excitement of the imagination with the sight of things excavated after centuries of burial. It formed a bridge from the present to the past. Biblical chronicles were no longer to me merely ancient religious history. They became the records of life of a people not unlike the Falashas."

Godfrey Higgins, an English expert on antiquities, says, "The Chaldees were originally Negroes."

XIV
An African Voyage to America

Abubakari was master of the world's largest empire. The Arabs said it was larger than all the civilized states of Europe, larger than the Holy Roman Empire. His empire was Mali, extending down to the northern deserts, to the southern jungles, east to the gold and copper mines of Takkeda and as far west as the sea waters of the Atlantic.

He was bored with no desires for pilgrimages, battles or conquests. He turned away from Koramic recitals and he could not adjust to the conservative ways of the Moslems. His mind was piqued with scholarly talk he had heard about a gourd-shaped world, of the big ocean to the west and a possible new world beyond that. The tales conflicted, but Abubakari listened. An old fisherman and an Arab sea captain insisted there were islands visited by North African sailors (the Canary Islands). They stood on the edge of the great ocean; the glassy sometimes turbulent ocean which could carry huge boats to a vast world far away.

Abu interviewed shipbuilders from Egypt and cities along the Mediterranean. He selected the coast of Senegambia for his boatbuilding. Carpenters, smiths, captains, caravan guides and men who knew the compass and other nautical instruments. Also assembled for the voyage to America were grain, merchants, potters, weavers, jewelers, magicians, diviners and thinkers.

The master plan said each vessel should tug its own supply boat; carrying gold for trade, dried meat, grain, preserved fruit in ceramic jars. The food should last for two years. All branches of the Mandingo military took part in these frantic but detailed preparations.

The convoy sailed away with Abubakari electing to stay behind. After a long wait, a lone sea captain returned. He said when the ships disappeared over the horizon, he did not follow.

Abubakari decided he would build a second fleet as complete as the first and that he would command it himself. He did. His personal flagship had a raised desk from which he could see enough of his

Abubakari, master of the world's largest empire.

give sound commands. Before sailing he passed rulership over brother Kankan Musa and sailed out the Senegal river west- toward the ocean. One hundred and eighty years before Columbus ned the Americas, Abubakari II eased into the Atlantic ocean held his position while his ships fanned out on each side in a voy as far as the eyes could see.

A drummer on key ships gave his position. All messages were ordinated by the king's flagship. The fleet remained in place while e navigators sought the current they had heard about. Finally, fac- ng the New World, Abubakari gave the word and they moved west- ward.

XV
Early Black Migrations

Anthropologists and archaeologists have found concrete evidence of the numerous mass migrations of Black people. Some took place long before the dawn of history. Blacks migrated to all parts of the known and unknown world. They sought agricultural lands, areas where live game could support them and grazing lands which could sustain their cattle. Visible remains have been found of Black inhabitation in Assyria, Southern Ireland, Malay Peninsula, France, Italy, Spain, Wales and the eastern archipelago. Carvings, statues and utensils and bones connected them with previous locations.

Other findings show Africans and people of African descent migrated to Japan, China, East Indies, Arabia and Asia Minor. They left traces in Turkey, Palestine, Greece and eastern Europe.Probably at a time when a land mass connected Africa to Europe, they went from Gibraltar into Spain, Portugal, France and England. Roman writers refer to a dark-skinned people they found in Wales and Western England as *silures*. The *picts* who lived in some of the British Isles were also of African descent. The Elamites of Persia, the Babylonians, Sumerians, Hittites, Sabaeans and the Phoenician-Carthagians had prominent African strains in their populations.

Sir Henry E. Johnston says early Egypt and Algeria possessed a Black population. Joseph Widnes' book, *Race and Life of the Aryan People*, claims the first people of ancient Babylon were Black.

The Grimaldi were a Black people who lived in Europe as early as twelve thousand years ago. Abundant evidence of their culture has been dug up in southern and central Europe. Two skeletons from this period were displayed at the Museum in Monaco.

Roland Burrage Dixon, Harvard University anthropologist and author of *The Radial History of Man* (1923), contends that "the presence of Negroes in Paleolithic time has been universally admitted on the northern Mediterranean coast. It continued to be a discernible factor in the population of Western Russia until the Middle Ages."

In his *Environment and Race*, published in London in 1927, Griffith Taylor said, "Next in order in Europe would seem to be the Negrito race of which more evidence is accumulating each year. We may label this fourth stratum, *Negroid*. These people must have been quite abundant in Europe toward the close of the Paleolithic period. Skulls in east Brazil (in South America) show where similar folk penetrated the New World."

XVI
Bilal, Aide to Mohammed

Bilal, an Ethiopian slave, became treasurer and first high priest of the Mohammedan Empire. Born about 600 A.D., Bilal was the Prophet's first convert. His full name was Hadzrat Bilal Ibn Rahab. His entry into the Islamic faith was nearly fatal. After his conversion his master tortured him almost to death. Mohammed saved his life by purchasing him and setting him free.

Bilal was nursed back to health and was made first muezzin, the holy man who called the faithful to prayer. The resulting friendship and respect between the two men carried them to earth-shaking heights and changed the destiny of Africa and the world. Comparisons of this deep relationship has been made to that of Peter and Jesus.

Bilal was a close companion to Mohammed in peace and in war, riding beside him with the drawn sword, striking out in the name of Allah. It is said, Mohammed thought so highly of Bilal he granted him precedence in heaven.

Nearing death, Mohammed offered the leadership of the empire to Bilal, but the African preferred his position and yielded to Abu Bek. Later he stepped aside for Omar the Great at whose side he rode after the capture of Jerusalem.

Bilal has been described as a tall, gaunt, Black man with bushy hair. His words and actions were inspirational. He could speak more fervently than anyone.

Another of Bilal's duties was to receive diplomats and distinguished guests. Once he was sent by Amru, the Mohammedan general, to meet with Prince Constantine, the Christian general. There were terms to be worked out about the possible capture of Syria. When the prince saw Bilal, he said he would have nothing to do with a Black slave. In return, Bilal saw that tougher terms were imposed on Constantine than Amru would have planned at first.

Bilal lived to be a hundred years old. He died singing a song, called the *Azan* which had been sung from the minarets, and little towers of the temples, calling the faithful to prayer. He was buried in the ancient city of Damascus where his tomb was a principal sight for visitors both Christian and Islamic.

Lafcadio Hearn, an international writer, said, "Bilal, the Black Abyssinian, whose voice was the mightiest and sweetest of Islam."

XVII
African Traders

Beyond 4000 B.C. until the Portuguese arrived in the 15th century A.D., Africans had carried on an extensive and varied trade among themselves and with industrious nations of the known world. During antiquity they traded with the Phoenicians who augmented the scope of trade. Blacks sailed across the Red Sea carrying gold, ivory and gum, doing business with Arabia and Egypt; then with Babylon and countries south of the Sudan.

The commerce with Babylon dates back to 2700 years before Christ.

Around 2500 B.C. Black Africans built hundreds of barges and flatboats which they sold to Egypt for her trade with Syria, Palestine and Crete.

It was during this period that Africans produced chairs and tables as we know them. They fashioned the brass claw feet which are seen on expensive European and American chairs. There were copies of similar feet on Egyptian furniture. Further, this period saw developed plaster, brick and stone rooms. They showed the skills and craftsmanship of Africans, as well as proportion, color and texture we admire today.

African Carthagians were expert traders of ivory, grain, purple dyes, and ostrich feathers. They did so with Mediterranean countries. The Black African Phoenicians of Carthage ventured and traded as far north as the British Isles. Dark-skinned men are said to have dug for lead and tin in the Carthaginian area near Cornwall, England. The Phoenician word *sack* was left as a part of the English language.

King Solomon sent his ships to the Black nations for products of their mines and forests.

These same Phoenician-Carthaginians, direct descendants of the Canaanites (the sons of Ham), visited Iceland where they learned of a vast continent beyond the sea, which was the New World.

Four hundred years after the siege of Carthaginian cities by the Romans in the second century before Christ, Indonesian and Malaysian vessels were sailing into Arabian and African ports. During this period, in East Africa, Bantu-speaking Africans traded and mingled with Persians, Arabs, Chinese, and, of course, the Malaysians and the Indonesians.

Much later, in the eighth century after Christ, ships from China came to Black African countries for rhinoceros horns, ivory, camphor, copper, sandalwood, gold and frankincense.

In the twelfth century African east coast cities witnessed scenes of spectacular trading with Middle East nations and countries of the Orient. Market places were a riot of colors and fragrances such as silks and brocades, Ming bowls and vases, Sung porcelains, copper, silver and gold jewelry from Sultanbas, fine carpets from the Middle East, exquisite mahogany and teak carvings from Indonesia and ivory figures from Canton. Africans wore their red fezzes and black merchants' caps, red shoes, turbans and native blue cotton garments.

The exciting glitter and spicy bustle of active and peaceful international commerce promoted deep and mutual civilizing influences. These prevailed until destruction arrived with the Portuguese in the fifteenth century.

XVIII
Ann Zingha, Warrior Queen of Angola

Ann Zingha, the fighting Queen of the Matamba in Angola was born around 1582 at the time when Portugal was seizing parts of her African country. She grew up impatiently, planning to do something about the brazenness of the invader. Patiently and thoroughly she recruited groups of Angolan women, told them her plan and their duty to throw the Portuguese out of their country. She trained them well and when the time was right she led her troops against the government soldiers from Portugal.

Battle after battle she won, much to the amazement of her enemies. She sought the aid of native chiefs and the Dutch and waged dogged and terrifying encounters against the Portuguese. There were many accounts by government soldiers of the fear they witnessed when they saw Ann on the field against them. After sixteen years Ann surrendered because her spears, bows and arrows were no match for European firearms.

Her personal warfare did not end with the cessation of hostilities. She harassed the authorities constantly. She refused an alliance with them, saying to the viceroy at Loanda that giving back the Portuguese prisoners was enough. When the treaty was finally signed, Ann let it be known she did not believe Portugal would keep it or respect the commitment.

Alternately Ann embraced Christianity, then rejected it. In later years, after unforgivable treatment by the Portuguese, she dropped the faith. The pleas of the missionaries and others fell on deaf ears. On the death of her sister (Ann herself had reached seventy years of age) she softened and accepted the faith again.

Although in her seventies, the queen exercised with weapons to maintain her health.

Ann fought until the end, showing constant and ever-increasing resentment against the Portuguese. After her death, she struck her last

Ann Zingha, Warrior Queen of Angola

ironic blow at the government and the church. She lay in state dressed in her royal robes, her hands clasping a bow and arrow.

IXX
Aesop, The Black Fabulist

Aesop, the world's most celebrated writer and narrator of fables, has been erroneously called a Greek fabulist. In reality he was a sixth century B.C. Samian Black slave.

Fables bearing his name have come down to modern times through scholars such as Phaedrus, a Macedonian freedman of Caesar Augustus. He wrote five books of Aesop's fables into verse. The collection of his prose fables was used all over Western Europe during the Middle Ages.

Maximus Planudes the Great, a leaned Greek scholar and fourteenth century monk, also owned a collection of Aesop's Fables. His research on Aesop goes further. He wrote of Aesop, "He was flat nosed. He had black skin from which he contracted his name, Aesop, being the same with Ethiop, or Ethiopian." Other great writers agreed with Planudes, including Cameraria, Osborn, Baudoin and Bellegrade.

The life of witty and caustic Aesop changed when he was purchased by one Xanthus at a market in Asia Minor. Little else is known except he was born of Ethiopian parents around 560 B.C. at Phrygia in Asia Minor. Aesop's quick thinking and unpredictability added excitement and challenge to his master's life.

Aesop both delighted and angered listeners with his satire and ironic wit.

His fate was additionally enriched when he talked King Croesus

Aesop, the Black Fabulist

of Lydia out of a war with his own Samian country. Croesus, the richest man in the world, was so impressed with Aesop he took him to his home and provided him with money and papers to travel. Aesop visited Egypt, Greece, Babylon, Asia and Corinth.

From six hundred years before Christ to this day some of the world's greatest scholars have been inspired and influenced by Aesop's works. These men include Plato, Aristotle, Aristophanes, Solon, Cicero, Caxton, Julius Caesar, and La Fontaine. Socrates spent his last days putting Aesop's fables into verse.

Aesop lived by his wit and his subtle and not-so-subtle fables. It is said that when he spoke before a group of natives of the city of Delphos in Greece, some became so angry they hurled him off a cliff.

XX

Black African Presence in America

There has been a change in scholarly attitudes on recognizing Black people and their very early presence in America. The phenomenal eleven colossal heads of Black Africans found in La Venta, San Lorenzo and Tres Zapotes in Mexico enjoy decreasing skepticism. The 1964 Barcelona meeting of the International Congress of Americanists agreed that African skeletons have been substantially reported in pre-Christian and medieval layers of diggings in America.

Peter Martyr d'Anghera, the first historian on America, tells of a meeting between Balboa and his Spanish explorers and the Blacks of Darien (Panama). This was in 1513. The Blacks lived a day's march up into the mountains from Quarequa. They had been shipwrecked and had made their own settlement in the mountains. They had become a fierce people. They were at war constantly with the Indians at Quarequa. They were captured in battle by the Indians, and they also took Indians captive. There has been no general revelation of these facts; however, these Blacks were the first to have been seen in the Indes. Among the Spanish shipwrecks of African vessels on the American coast were nothing new.

Some solid examples of pre-Columbian Black African presence in America are clay, gold and stone portraiture showing Black African strain. These were unearthed in Central and South America. Some of the unmistakable African resemblance has been dated from 800 to 700 B.C.

It has been confirmed that Abubakari II, Emperor of the Kingdom of Mali did reach America with some of his 2000 vessels in 1310. The last of the pre-Columbian potters, the Mixtecs, have left behind clay sculptures of African faces which include the flared nostrils, the bone formation of the cheeks and the darkened grain of the skin. Some include the Gambian earrings which can be definitely tied to that sub-community of early Ghana and later Mali. Cadamosto saw the earrings on warrior boatmen in Africa. Clothing, jewelry and various artifacts attest the Black presence in Mexico. Among these have been found the caduceus, an upright design of entwined serpents. This was a religious symbol in ancient Kush and was adopted by the Egyptians. Physicians in America associate this symbol with their profession.

Peruvian records and tradition tell of Black men coming from the east and conquering the Andes mountains. Terracottas with Negroid faces, denoting varying pre-Columbian periods, are scattered throughout South and Central America.

There is evidence of Black Africans appearing in Mexico just before and after Christ and of the Olmecs and the Aztecs venerating Blacks as deities.

A priest of the Dominican Order, Gregoria Garcia, spent nine years in Peru in the fifteen hundreds. He mentions an island off Cartagena, Columbia, as the first point of encounter between Blacks and the Spanish explorers in the New World.

Both Darien (Panama) and Columbia lie within the end currents which moved swiftly and forcefully from Africa to America. This can well account for early purposeful and unplanned landings of Africans.

Alphonze de Quatrefages, anthropologist at the Museum of National History in Paris, identified in his book *The Human Species* (1905) that Black inhabitants were found in small numbers and isolated areas in America. Some examples were the Jamassi of Florida, The Charus of Brazil, the Black Caribs of Saint Vincent on the Gulf of Mexico and the Black Zuni of present-day Arizona and Mexico.

In Columbus' *Journal of the Third Voyage* he said he wanted to find out about the Black people the Indians had told him about. Indians were found farming yams and taro, an African food, while the Portuguese explorers in Africa saw natives cultivating maize, an American Indian product.

PART II

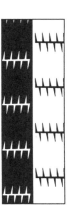

I
Before the Dawn of History

During recent history Blacks have been identified only with Africa. The knowledge that Blacks made extensive migrations to far away parts of the world for many centuries has been hidden, de-emphasized or diverted. Actually there is evidence even before written history that Blacks were world travelers.

Scholars in this century have been able to find concrete and abundant evidence for numerous Black colonies outside Africa. There were Blacks on the Australian continent when it was first sighted by the Spanish in 1604—Australia is 8000 miles from Africa. American World War II servicemen were greeted by Blacks on the Solomon Islands off New Guinea—again thousands of miles from Africa. The *Nakis*, a colony of Blacks, were discovered in 1923 in southern China by Dr. Joseph Rock, a representative of the United States Department of Agriculture. On the Adamese Islands, a part of the Republic of India, descendants of *Negrito* people have been found. Though few are aware of it, Blacks have inhabited the Philippines for hundreds of years.

Movements of Blacks in pre-history provides new insights into their contributions to the Old World and the New World.

It is well supported that Blacks were the first human beings on earth and it is possible that during their migrations throughout the unknown world, they helped lay the framework of civilization. In the Western Hemisphere, Indians, or *Native Americans*, followed Black Asians across the Bering Straits. They found the Blacks prospering in a society more viable than their own. As happened in the other hemisphere and on other prehistoric continents, there were killings, warfare and intermarriage for thousands of years until the Blacks were finally extinct. Skeletal remains of Blacks unearthed in Central America, South America and in Arizona predate the Zuni Indians.

The African earth has surrendered to archaeologists and anthropologists the earliest remains of man and his ancestors. Man originated in Africa. Scholars have dug up skeletons in Africa as old as 175,000 years, while sites in Europe including Italy, England, Russia and Scandinavia have yielded bones no more than 20,000 years old.

Proof of Black habitation has been uncovered in Western Asia. Discoveries dating back 6,000 years before Christ show Black Settlers called *Natufians* in Palestine. Gerald Massey, a French anthropologist, claims that "the sole race that can be traced among the aborigines all over the earth, or below it, is the dark race of *Negrito* type." Prehistoric India was occupied by Blacks who were followed by the pre-Dravidians and later the Dravidians. Blacks were indigenous peoples of pre-historic China, Japan, Asia, Australia and the Islands of the Pacific 50,000 years ago. The fossil remains, artifacts uncovered and the art left to scholars strongly suggest that prehistoric Black families perfected the first foundation of civilization.

There is no question today about Black involvement in prehistoric and ancient Egypt, first known as Kemit meaning "land of the Blacks." The Blacks in Cush (Ethiopia) and Egypt developed the first society governed by laws, structured systematic religion, and planted and nurtured the seeds of the world's greatest civilization.

Babylon was founded and maintained by Blacks. The ancient people of Sumeria have been referred to as Assyric-Babylonian and have been described as people with shaven heads and Black faces.

Ancient Chinese text suggests that Blacks laid the foundation of civilization there. J. A. Rogers in his *Sex and Race*, said "Blacks penetrated into the far north of China and showed themselves in the face of the Tarter." Black civilizations were found in India, in the valleys of the Indus River and the Ganges River. The Ganges River was named after an Ethiopian general who carried his conquest of India to that point.

The Black Grimaldis were the major inhabitants and the rulers of Europe for tens of thousands of years. They produced the first known art and invented the technique for sculpture. The statue of the Venus of Willendorf was made by the Grimaldies.

Irish folklore mentions small Black people, called the *Firbolg*. Gerald Massey, Godfrey Higgins and David MacRitchie, all British writers, have written about ancient Blacks in England and Ireland. Ancient Welsh folk tales also mention Black people. England and Spain were included in the migrations of Blacks. After these thousands of years of surviving and being extinguished, of creating and inventing, Blacks came into the dawn of history with more to offer than any other group of people on earth.

II

Hatshepsut, First Queen of Egypt

Hatshepsut was an Egyptian princess whose grandmother, Nefertari Aahmes, was an Ethiopian. She lived more than 150 years before Tutankhamen, or approximately 3500 years ago.

Early in her royal life, Hatshepsut challenged 3000 years of male supremacy by fighting her way to the throne and holding it for 33 years. She named Nehusi, a full-blooded Black, as prime minister and another Black, Semnut, as chief architect. It was with the latter that she campaigned to build the greatest and most beautiful temple Egypt had ever seen. Today her temple at Dier el Bahari stands as a monument to her effort and the genius of her builders. Much of the life of this aggressive Black woman is inscribed on the walls of this magnificent structure.

In her defense against prevailing anti-women attitudes, Hatshepsut startled her opponents by announcing she was a man. She dressed in male clothing and officially declared she was of virgin birth. She assumed the manly title of Chief Spouse of Amen, The Mighty One.

The expedition to Punt led by Hatshepsut 1500 years before Christ was historic as well as exciting. She took her prime minister, her architect and her young daughter, Nafrura. She loaded 300 vessels of gold, incense, incense-bearing trees, myrrh and many animals strange to her native Egypt.

A matter of breeding, not race, plagued the queen. The opposition resented that she was not of pure Theban stock. As stated, her grandmother was Ethiopian and her family's roots went back to the Sudan.

She ruled effectively until her death and was buried in the Valley of the Kings, a fact unheard of until this time. She was the only woman buried there and the first identifiable Black woman to rule Egypt.

According to British archaeologist Sir John Garstang, Hatshepsut was the princess who reared Moses.*

III

Akhnaton, Believer in One God

During the Eighteenth Egyptian Dynasty, actually in 1350 B. C., Akhnaton was king, or Pharaoh, of this great nation. History will remember him as more than a king or head of state. He was of African descent, a serious philosopher and the first ruler on earth to believe in one god. He opposed all of the Egyptians who had preceded him on the throne and who believed in many gods. Some of these Gods

* The New York Times, January 27, 1932

had been borrowed from the Black Africans in the south.

Akhnaton was the son of Amenophis and grandson of Thutmose III who was of mixed blood and quite African in appearance. His mother was a Black woman, Queen Tiyi.

Akhnaton behaved compulsively about his one god theology. He risked everything in an attempt to convert his people to the one god theory. Instead, his citizens resisted him. The people wanted conquests and the spoils of war, not peace.

Akhnaton is well known, too, because of his beautiful wife, Nefertiti. There are hundreds of Egyptian paintings and ancient stories of her great beauty. European historians, even those who tried to rearrange Black history, had to admit she was the most beautiful woman of her time.

The king wanted a son, but beautiful Nefertiti gave him seven daughters. He could have taken another wife to give him a son. He did not do this. He lived with Nefertiti.

The *one god* theory which Akhnaton lived by and preached disturbed his followers throughout his kingdom. He had inherited a vast empire. His direct and indirect control of Egypt extended into Babylonia, Cicilia, Cyprus, Crete, Syria and Palestine. However, his one god theory did not suit the aggressive mood of the times.

In a period which cried for action, Akhnaton wrote beautiful hymns in praise of his one god. To him his god was a formless deity. Hundreds of years before Moses wrote the forbidding commandments banishing engraven images, Akhnaton had already spoken out against them. While Moses claimed his god was jealous, Akhnaton's god was one of perfect love, compassionate, sympathetic and feeling—even toward the chicken that "crieth in the eggshell."

Records show that no other monarch controlled so much and so many with such sensitivity. He stated that his god gave the manchild a mother "to soothe him so that he might not weep."

There are similarities between the scriptures and the creations of Akhnaton. He is quoted as saying, "the kingdom of God is within you," long before Jesus did.

More than 300 years before David was born, Akhnaton wrote psalms which sounded exactly like David's Chapter 104 in the Bible.

There is evidence that the peaceful, revolutionary Egyptian king wrote psalms in the fourteenth century before Christ.

Some historians contend that Moses was influenced by Akhnaton's preachings or by the knowledge of them, and that he took up the theory and preached it before the Israelites.

Thus the son of an outstanding southern monarch and a Sudanese Nubian mother, left his mark on the minds of men more than a thousands years before Christ was born.

IV
Tut, Black Boy King

The treasures of King "Tut" have dazzled millions of viewers throughout the world. Six hundred priceless artifacts from his tomb have been on traveling display including jewels and golden ornaments taken from his grave in Egypt by the British in 1922 after 3200 years of burial. These items of staggering value tell graphically of the splendor of the times in which young Tutankhamen lived thirteen hundred years before the birth of Jesus Christ. Little is told of Tutankhamen himself, of the little nine-year-old boy who ascended the throne of the mightiest nation on earth and died after nine years of rule.

Unbiased historians have made efforts to be impartial in trying to slash though the mystery and the biased writings of Europeans who researched and wrote about ancient Egypt. After tunneling through a maze of reports on the racial identity of Tutankhamen, they have decided he was a Black boy king in Egypt from 1361 to 1352 B. C.

Tutankhamen was a Pharaoh during nine years of the most famous of dynasties—the Eighteenth, which lasted from 1567 to 1320 B. C. The names of its rulers are legend or immortal in history.

Tut, whose real name was Tutankhamen, was a black boy of mighty Egypt. He died at age 18 after serving eight years.

In this dynasty there were names like Ahmose I, Nefertiti, the world's most beautiful woman and Queen Tiyi, the Black Sudanese grandmother of Tutankhamen. Others included Thutmose I, Thutmose II, Amenhotep II, Amenhotep III, Queen Hatshepsut the Great, and Akhnaton, the father of young Tutankhamen.

After his coronation, Tutankhamen assumed control with strong counsel over a highly centralized government with its capital at Thebes. This was a city heavily influenced by central Black African culture and history. His officers controlled an efficient civil service system, a flawless tax collecting procedure and the best diplomatic corps in the world. Mail and message distribution connected every nook and cranny of the huge empire. The Egyptian army and navy consisted of 20,000 men.

Tutankhamen followed the rules set down for him by marrying Ankhsenpaaten, one of the seven daughters of beautiful Nefertiti.

He ruled from Upper Egypt which was more closely identified with Black Africa to the south than Lower Egypt was, with its gates to the Mediterranean trade routes that the Asians used. Much later, during the Twenty-Fifth Dynasty, when Black African kings ruled as pharaohs, Thebes was also maintained as the capital. This dynasty began in 700 B. C., and it was at Thebes where Black rule was finally overcome.

The boy king took foreign policy seriously. He realized he had to rely on the great traditions of Egypt if his monitors abroad were to function and commerce was to be profitably maintained. He drew up special peace treaties with the Hittites and the Land of Kheta. His treaties on commerce were detailed to assure Egypt the greater portion of raw materials in her dealings with other nations. He kept his economy stable when he prevented skilled workers from leaving Egypt, since such an exodus would cripple the commerce of his country. One such treaty with the Hittites read:

> *If skilled men of the provinces go to the Hittites, the latter shall not receive them, but will return them to the Sun Lord of Justice.*

Tutankhamen showed deep and active interest in Nubia, which indicated the importance of this Black nation in world affairs. He appointed a Prince of Cush (Ethiopia) to the high rank of viceroy over Nubia.

Hui is mentioned as this viceroy. He was considered the second most powerful man in the king's cabinet. We can measure how important Hui was to the king by Hui's burial—more artifacts describing Tutankhamen's reign were found in Hui's tomb than in the king's own grave.

There are records which show that Tutankhamen received and lavishly entertained the Nubian officers and diplomats who came to visit him. He had further involvement with the Nubians as the result of an emotional experience. It was caused by the murder of his good Nubian friend and future god, Osiris, by Set, the dead man's brother. Tutankhamen mourned with Osiris' Black wife, Isis. He helped collect the many pieces of the slain man's body to be distributed to the scores of towns and cities which loved him and worshipped him.

Strikes among workers plagued the king from time to time. They happened when pay was late, depleted or withheld. Tutankhamen always appointed a priest to deal with the strikers. Workers were usually paid the first day of the month, and pay consisted of wheat, oil and durra (Egyptian corn).

Among the most difficult problems the young king assumed from his father and predecessor was one of religion. There was turmoil because of the controversial *one god* pressure put on the people by Akhnaton. It seems that Akhnaton was under the influence of the central African religion, which had held the *one god* theory for thousands of years. Its ideas Akhnaton had tried to impose on the people of the empire. In doing so, he had angered the priests of Amon, the god of gods. However, history credits Tutankhamen with restoring the old religion to Egypt.

On the way to his coronation, young Tutankhamen was apprehensive about the reception he might receive at the capital city of Thebes. Akhnaton had not only angered the priests, he had persecuted some. Tutankhamen was afraid of these men, since the priests would perform the coronation.

He grew up at the palace of his grandfather Amenophis III, at Amarna. He returned there to spend many official hours. He received his generals, ambassadors and notables at this serene spot. He has been described as sitting motionless, a glittering figure with his chest hidden under cascades of golden necklaces and his thin legs showing through the pleated white gauze.

A visit to the civil and criminal courts was a regular task of the kings. In a large, open room, judges, defendants, scribes and clerks sat in a circle. Trials in Egypt at this time were serious civil and religious matters. Tutankhamen always stopped by the president of the court with the firm observation, "I am with the kings of justice."

Historians agree that Tutankhamen was sickly. He suffered from constant headaches, chest pains and severe pains in the eyes.

V

Candaces of Ethiopia

Some of the greatest field generals of the ancient world were empresses of Ethiopia. One was a contemporary of Alexander the Great, the Macedonian. She was formidable Queen Candace. Her fame as a military tactician and field commander preceded her throughout the known world.

Legends have it that Alexander the Great, the mighty conqueror of all the armies he met, finally marched up to the border of Ethiopia and Egypt. For some reason he did not elect to fight Candace. The reason may have been that up to three centuries before Christ, Romans and other Mediterranean people had access only to hearsay about the mysteries of Africa below Egypt. The great general might have overestimated the unseen power hidden in the interior. Certainly he would not risk defeat by a woman and take a chance on spoiling his perfect record. Historians agree that Alexander and Candace had a pleasant visit. This meeting was in 332 B. C. at the first Cataract of the Nile.

There is mild confusion among some readers of history regarding the number of Candaces which appear throughout periods of Ethiopian history. It was a dynastic name which was adopted by Sudanese queens. It honored the name of the great military leader and queen who met with the undefeated Alexander the Great.

There was another Queen Candace. This one was from Meriotic Sudan. She shook the world with her daring also by riding before her armies in the face of overwhelming odds. Much later she faced legions of Augustus Caesar a few years before Christ was born. This engagement took place after Augustus had conquered Egypt and had pushed his legions to the Ethiopian border. Candace lost an eye in this battle, yet her courage and determination commanded the respect of Augustus. When Candace sent a list of demands to Caesar who had retired to the shores of the Mediterranean, he agreed to all of them. Her scorn of death and her unmatched bravery won the admiration of the world. A chauvinist writer was later to pen, "The queen had courage above her sex."

Still another fight with the Romans took place in 22 B. C. when Candace made battle with the Roman governor of Egypt. Again her defeat was severe. This time the Romans crossed the Ethiopian border and sacked the capital city of Napata. The reverend temple of Piankhy, the former Nubian King of Egypt, was also destroyed.

This might have been the same Candace mentioned in the Bible (Acts 8:27-29), when a eunuch in her service was baptized by Philip.

VI
Makeda, Queen of Sheba

Of the several serious stories about Makeda, the beautiful Black Queen of Sheba, the best is from the Ethiopian *Kebar Nagast*, or Glory of Kings. This one stands out mainly because the legend of the love affair between Makeda and King Solomon of Judea gave Ethiopia its remarkable cultural link and historical tie with Solomon and Israel.

Makeda was the heiress to a dynasty formed from a political split around 1370 B. C., more than three centuries before her birth. It is certain she performed queenly chores other than meeting with Solomon. However, it is this story alone which has persisted for more than three thousand years. This political love story can be seen from at least three viewpoints—the Ethiopian, the Arabian and the Biblical.

Tamrin, an Ethiopian merchant of some status and experience, was the first to really convince Makeda that the mighty kingdom of Solomon and his unmatched wisdom should not be missed. Makeda left it to Tamrin, who had been previously sought out by Solomon, to buy some of the "red gold of Emu," to lead her caravan to Jerusalem. This caravan of 787 asses and mules was laden with precious jewels, spices, fragrances and gold. It would be valued at three and a half million dollars on today's market.

After presenting her gifts to the king, Makeda entered the royal household which was both spectacular and unique. There were 700 wives, all of whom were princesses. Some were very famous royalty and daughters of well-known kings. Whether competition and personal involvement were initially considered by the Black queen, she must have weighed giving offense to the presence of Emmah, daughter of Achbal, King of Cyeon; Terada, daughter of the King of Sidon; Rachael, daughter of Hiram II, King of Tyre; Salimit, daughter of the King of Suman; and Nitocris, daughter of the King of Egypt. To add to Makeda's probable wonder, Solomon had 300 concubines. It must have dismayed them when the king showered most of his attention on Makeda during her visit.

The legends vary as to the marriage or the non-marriage between Queen Makeda and King Solomon. However, she did decide to return to her own country with a plan to teach the king's religion to her people in Sheba. Prior to her leaving, they became lovers. Makeda barely reached the borders of her kingdom when her son was born. She called him, "son of the wise man." Later the son of Solomon and Makeda was to be named Menelik I.

Classical painting, music, drama and literature from ancient times to today have told and retold versions of the legends. The Ethiopians have forty paintings of Makeda.

The Bible suggests that Makeda apologized for her blackness to the daughters of Jerusalem, but the Ethiopian version does not mention this.

It is possible that Makeda was of mixed blood, Ethiopian and Arab, which might account for an Arabian version of the story as well. Both the Bible and the Koran carry the legend of Sheba's the queen and King Solomon.

VII

Scientists and Builders

It has been very unfortunate that many European and American researchers have strongly implied that Africans invented nothing and explored nothing. These implications have blended naturally with the standard and historical stereotypes, prejudices and misleading writings. Even liberal writers have given the Africans credit for having only a *limited and simple technology*.

However, the reliable techniques of carbon-dating, along with recent discoveries, may discredit some of the incorrect statements on

West Africa perfected the refinement of steel to the point that it could be used for surgical instruments.

the African technology by biased writers, archaeologists and anthropologists. The often-used words such as *primitive* and *sub-social* may have to be retracted.

Recent discoveries have proved that African cultures achieved levels of technical development comparable with, or superior to, European cultures.

The embalming or mummification technique did not originate with the Egyptians. It began with the Black Nubians. (Even though the Egyptians were Black, too.) This closely guarded technique, which still remains a mystery, followed other Cushite contributions which flowed up the Nile to Egypt. During an expedition, a Professor F. Mori found the remains of an African child in Southwest Libya. The remains could be dated back to 3500 B. C., two centuries before the first Egyptian kingdom. The child's body was preserved and bound in the same manner as those of the pharaohs found later in Egypt.

The first Babylonians were Black, without question. Ancient literature has made dramatic references to Babylonian ships. As they sailed through the night, their masts were illuminated with *cold lights*. The phrase rules out fire light of any kind. Cold light would be more closely associated with battery-powered light.

Recently, Peter Schmidt, an anthropologist, and his companion, metallurgist Donald Avery, went among the Haya people of Tanzania. They found proof that Africans were producing medium carbon steel in preheated, forced draft furnaces over 2000 years ago. When Africans were forced by social, civil and natural circumstances to stop this advanced process, it was not rediscovered and practiced for 19 hundred years until German-born metallurgist Karl Wilhelm Siemens produced the same high-grade carbon steel.

To further support the existence of this highly advanced process, scholars have studied natives in the Lake Victoria region of Tanzania whose oral tradition describes the existence of prehistoric iron smelting. Some of the Africans accompanied the researchers to the sites of ancient furnaces and showed them how the heat was built up and maintained, a process far superior to the technique Europeans had accomplished.

Medieval West Africans devised metal implements so delicately refined they could be used by surgeons to perform surgery on the eyes, especially for the removal of cataracts.

One of the *marvels* Greek historian Herodotus mentioned during his tour of Egypt was the practice of medicine. No doctor was allowed a general practice. Each had to specialize. There were specialists for eyes, nose, ears, throat, intestines, stomach, teeth and the head. There were stringent sanitary laws which regulated the diagnosis and treatment of ailments. The method of capping teeth was a general procedure. In the first part of this book, Imhotep, Black physician to Zoser, King of Egypt, was discussed. He treated 200 known ailments.

In northwestern Kenya, as early as 300 B. C., Black Africans built an astronomical site at Namoratuntga. An accurate, complex, prehistoric calendar was devised. It was based on perfect astronomical alignments. When researchers recently climbed the eastern edge of Losidak Range at the Lake Turkana basin, they found 19 basalt pillars arranged in patterns which related to the position of certain stars and constellations.

It is a remarkable coincidence that they relate to the ancient Eastern Cushite calendar. This calendar was based on the rising of seven stars and constellations in conjunction with various phases of the moon. The calendar was calculated on a 364-day year of 12 months.

There is no question as to the professionalism of African builders. Recent discoveries in the Lake Chad region of West Africa have revealed deserted towns and cities. These areas were inhabited by hundreds, even thousands of people, probably thousands of years ago. There were temples, public buildings, palaces and memorials. All evidence shows these were built by people of great skill.

The miraculous stone towers of Zimbabwe show the artistry of their brick masons. The bricks were uniquely crafted with 12-corners of 12 sides and were laid symmetrically in triangular geometric forms, without mortar in a single joint or in a single layer. This is similar to the slab fitting of the old Egyptian pyramids. There were openings for ventilation in these Zimbabwian structures. Today towers stand in that country as physical testimony to the genius of its architects, builders and engineers and the scientific knowledge among them. Their superior techniques of architecture and building were enhanced by their ability to solve problems. They considered the weight of a building they constructed, along with the water levels below it, so that the water could support the structure. This knowledge of hydrographics further illustrates the skills of Zimbabwe.

Ancient Ghana was known for the extensive weaving of cloth. It was a skill handed down for hundreds of years from father to son. As late as the 18th Century, Kente cloth, which was to become famous, was first woven by Nana Tolh. The cloth became a symbol of royalty during the Denkyira Dynasty in 1741. During this time, the Ashanti were the dominant West African nation.

An ancient Nubian incense burner has been found on the Nile between Egypt and the Sudan. It has been carbon-dated at 3500 B.C. which precedes any organized Egyptian kingdom. Inscriptions on the burner indicate direct Sudanese influences on ancient Egypt. The crowned insignia and royal insignia, which later appeared in Egypt, were found on the incense burner.

When Count Christian Volney of France saw the Egyptians in 1785, he said that the Black people being enslaved in Europe and America were of the same color and characteristics of the Egyptians tilling the fields of Egypt, and that these were the people who had passed great civilization and culture down to the present through the Greeks, Romans and Europeans. Clearly Blacks contributed to Egyptian culture.

Therefore, some of the scientific accomplishments of the Egyptians might be added to the list. These included a method of hatching eggs without the hen, a process of dyeing cloth, staining materials, and using metallic oxides to change hues and produce colors which they applied to glass and porcelain.

Africans were *not* minor technologists.

VIII
Blacks in Mythology

Before Romulus, the son of Mars and a vestal virgin, founded Rome in 735 B.C., long before Homer recited, Greece was in its early childhood and while the world was young, the ancient capital of Cush was thriving along the Nile River. (Cush is the other name for ancient Ethiopia.)

Classic literature has many references to Blacks and Ethiopians which put them in a most favorable and revered light.

It seems Ethiopia was mentioned more than any other nation. Most of the gods of Greece were of Egyptian origin. The Egyptians were Black and Egypt has been described as a daughter of Ethiopia. Herodotus, the most famous, most quoted and thorough Greek historian said, "Almost all of the names of gods came into Greece from Egypt."

Zeus, acclaimed father of all the gods, was of Ethiopian ancestry. He sired a mulatto son named Epaphus. Famed Aschylus, tragic Greek poet, said of Zeus, "And thou shall bring forth Black Epaphus, thus named from the manner of Zeus engendering." One of the titles of Zeus was Ethiop, which meant Black.

The goddess Diana of Attica was Black and Ethiopian. It was the great Apollo who took her away from her country. Also, it was at the Greek city of Corinth where a Black Venus was adored and worshipped. Evidently African women were the favorites of Greek poets. One such poet has been quoted as saying, as he praised an African woman, "With her charms Didymee has ravished my heart. Alas I melt as wax at the sight of her beauty. She is Black, it is true, but what matters? Coals are black; but when they are alight they glow like rose cups." Some writers contend that ancient Greeks chose an African princess to represent Minerva, their goddess of wisdom.

When the Greeks attacked the city ruled by Agamemnon, it was saved by troops of Blacks. The King of Egypt helped out by sending ten thousand Ethiopians to relieve the city. Also the Black Virgin,

Isis, was worshipped many centuries after the advent of Christianity. Processions to her honor marched through the streets of Rome as late as 394 A.D.

The selection of Eurybates, who was Black skinned and wooly haired, as the herald for Odysseus showed the respectful consciousness of Black power on the edge of the Greek world. The same was true for Northern Africa. All along its edges, Black migrations and rulers affected this dynamic, innovative nation whose world contributions have yet to be justly appreciated.

An established Greek settlement in Egypt called Naukratis gave Greeks direct contact with Black people and by the sixth century B.C., contemporary literature revealed a keen awareness of Blacks. Ethiopians are found in Homer's *Illiad* and *Odyssey*, as well as in the works of Euripides, Herodotus, Aeschylus and Hesiod. William Leo F. Hansberry says that, "Traditions preserved in the poems of the epic cycle, through the Memnon legend, connected the royal house of Ethiopia with the royal houses of Persia and Homeric Troy."

Many hundred years before Homer's day, Ethiopians were in direct contact with Aegean people. However, it was Homer who stressed that Black Ethiopians were the dominant people in India, Asia and in their own land in the West. At the dawn of European literature, Homer and Hesiod frequently referred to African lands and their *dusky* inhabitants. After the Age of Pericles, the fifth century before Christ, classical literature reached its peak. Ethiopia and its people were favorite and familiar topics with the leading poets, historians and geographers.

The literature of Olympadorus, Stephanus of Byzantium, and Helidorus strove to keep the historical prominence and the romantic tales of Ethiopia alive, even though the glory of Greece and the grandeur of Rome loomed over them.

Ethiopia in poetic tradition outranked that of Egypt, despite its long list of well-known names. The Black culture of Ethiopia has enjoyed its recognition much longer.

IX
Influence on the Greeks

The influence of African culture, history and tradition can be traced through Egypt and North Africa. It can be seen in the very beginnings of Grecian civilization. Homer's Odyssey XIX tells of the glories of Ethiopia. Africans were called the *favorites of the gods* and *the most just of men*.

According to Dr. William Metford, in his book *History of Greece*, there were Ethiopian colonies in Greece. This led him to doubt whether Greeks were of Phoenician or Egyptian origin. He described Greece as a melting pot of nations and noted that the engravings and wall paintings in both the Aurignacian and Magdelian Ages were similar to those of modern Blacks.

Sir Arthur Evans has said that in the new dawn of history the Greeks were not pale-skinned northerners, but a dark-haired, brown complexioned race.

The famous and revered Oracle of Delphi had Negroid features. History remembers the Ethiopian king from Meroe who came to aid the Trojans in the defense of Troy in the thirteenth century before Christ.

The Black slaves among the Greeks shared more in common with the Greeks than did white captives from Central Europe and Asia. Precious works of Greek art, such as coins and cameos, depicted Black faces and Blacks engaged in activity.

At a time in history when early Greeks were savages and feasted on the human flesh of their enemies, Africans in Egypt and Ethiopia had obtained a very high level of civilization.

George Wells Parker claims that the great Greek years were due to African influence. To connect this period of Greek history with Black history, we had seals of Queen Tiyi, the Sudanese grandmother of Tutankhamen, and Axamenophis III, his grandfather. These seals described the Greek civilization and also told of the Blacks who educated the Greeks. During this same period, the influence of Black

culture reached the Greek Islands of Cr
can be recognized in the ancient art o
and stories telling of a Black Minoan c
Black soldiers.

Some African figures were worshi
They appear as gods in Greek Mytholo

The title of Zeus, the greatest of go

Aristotle said that the Egyptians
Ethiopians had wooly hair.

The cultivation of the olive and the use of bees to obtain honey and wax were taken to Greece by an Egyptian named Arustaemens. Thucydides claims that Attica was founded by an African named Cecrops. It was a very early province of Greece and it was here that the earliest strides toward civilization in Greece were made.

Cecrops also introduced marriage, law, government and religion. The famous Greek historian Herodotus says Egyptians taught Greeks the theory of the universality of the soul. Armed with this new knowledge, Greeks began to migrate to Egypt.

There were mechanical inventions attributed to Archimedes the Greek, including the endless screw and the hydraulic screw used to pump water. These had already been used in Egypt for a thousand years.

Great Greek scholars and scientists taught by Black Africans and Egyptians included Thales of Miletus, Pythagoras of Samos, Archimedes of Sicily, Diodorus, Homer, Solon, Aristotle and Lycurgas. According to the Greek biographer, Plutarch, the Egyptians liked Pythagoras and delighted in teaching him.

The Goddess Diana of Attica was Ethiopian. It was Apollo, the Sun God, who took her away from Ethiopia. At Corinth, in Greece, a Black Venus was worshipped.

The Greeks and the Romans admired the Africans as leaders of culture. No people in antiquity doubted that Blacks were the fathers of civilization.

Euphorus (405 B.C.) was so impressed that he called them the most mighty and numerous people of the known world. Solon, a contemporary of Plato, traveled in Egypt. There was great mutual respect between the Greek and the Egyptian scholars.

earned the value and use of an occupational direc- Egyptians. In this instance, every town kept a book of hich was listed every citizen with a description of his job upation. Solon took this idea back to Greece.

ignificant impressions of Egypt and Black Africa among the Greeks ere numerous. Herodotus said, "That country contains more wonders than any other country and may vie with all the other regions in the works it exhibits, admirable beyond the powers of description."

Diodorus says, "Egypt excels all other places in magnificent structures." Philostrates referred to Blacks as "Charming Ethiopians with wooly hair."

Democrates learned astrology in Egypt and the Greeks learned agriculture and letters from the Egyptians. Telecles and Theodorus learned sculpture.

X

Among the Romans

From before the beginning of the Punic Wars (264 B.C.), through Rome's mightiest years until its decline, Blacks had had an active role in Roman society. They were citizens, soldiers, military leaders, teachers, writers, slaves, chariot drivers and racers and artisans. It was a century after the Third Punic War (149-146 B.C.) before Rome began to know about the interior of Africa. Until then, all information came from countries which bordered West Africa such as Carthage and Egypt. Later Romans penetrated into the interior for trade, battle, losses and conquests.

Records show that a Roman official named Cornelius Gallus met with an Ethiopian government official in 29 B.C. to settle a boundary dispute which would separate Roman Egypt from Ethiopia. Seven years later, a strong Ethiopian army contingent routed a Roman garrison in Upper Egypt, threw down revered statues and carried off some of the pieces. In retaliation, Rome's Gaius Petronius stormed into the Cushite country, laying waste cities and towns in his path. He damaged the sacred temple of Piankhy the first Black African Pharaoh of the Twenty-Fifth Dynasty, and sacked the mighty Cushite city of Napata.

Romans designed, printed and distributed coins bearing African heads during the reign of Caesar Augustus. They were used until the fourth century after Christ.

Roman scholar Pliny the Elder (23-79A.D.), wrote graphically about his observations of Roman trade in Ethiopia: "Our only intercourse is the trade in the precious stone imported from Ethiopia which we call carbuncle." Greek geographer Strabo, a century earlier, had mentioned Ethiopia as the site for *carbuncle*.

The great sport of Romans involving wild animals could not have been possible without the hunting skill and business acumen of Black Africans. Rome required wild animals, unmaimed and in perfect health, for its games. Thus tigers and lions were shipped to Rome from Africa.

There were at least two Black African-born Roman generals. One of them, the Sudanese Septimius Severus is said to have become Emperor of Rome. He gained more African land for the Romans by marching his armies into the gateway of the Sahara. He died in Britain as head of a fighting Roman army of occupation. Lucius Quietus was also a Sudanese. His major service was under Emperor Marcus Ulpius Trajanus (98-117 A.D.). He was sent to put down a rebellion of the Jews. African soldiers also served in the legions of Diocletian and Justinian. At the end of the long, costly war with Carthage, Rome shipped thousands of Carthaginian soldiers back to Rome to fight in her legions.

Researchers have revealed the similarity of the beads found in Ashanti graves to those found in the ruins at Pompeii and at the bottom of the Thames River in London, England.

During the siege of the Egyptian city of Alexandria by Caesar Augustus, Cleopatra the Queen, planned to send her children by

Julius Caesar and Marcus Antony to a friendly queen "in the hope that in Ethiopia they could find shelter and support against Rome." This showed the respect held for Ethiopia by both Egypt and Rome. Her conqueror was the same Caesar Augustus who often played marbles in Rome with African children.

Emperor Nero ordered an expedition into Ethiopia before his death in 68 A.D. Although Meroe, the great former capital city of Cush, was decayed by then, there was positive evidence that there had been many magnificent buildings. It is now known that four thousand artisans had worked in this hub of industrial growth.

It was only 88 years earlier that the Ethiopian Queen Candace made direct war against Caesar Augustus. She was defeated, but won an honorable peace. There are some reports that she lost an eye in the fight. This Candace* had ruled from Upper Egypt and had resided at Meroe.

XI
Black Emperor of Rome

Septimius Severus was born in Africa in an area known as Tripolitania. It was his boyhood ambition to go to Rome and join one of its superior military forces. He was born a Roman citizen and spoke his native Punic and Latin.

As the years passed, Septimius worked his way to the highest rank in the Roman army, that of counsul or general. He commanded a crucial Claudian camp at Valkenburg in southern Holland at the mouth of the Rhine River. Later he was the Roman Governor in the area,

*This was a dynastic name.

Septimus Severus, Roman Consul in Germany and Emporer of Rome, was a native of Africa.

where he lived in a mansion once occupied by Emperor Marcus Aurelius. Marcus wrote his famous and classic *Meditations* there. The governor's mansion was fitted with glass windows, radiant heat and floors made of marble from Syria and Greece.

It was from Germany that Septimius rose to the office of Emperor of mighty Rome. His troops supported him, thus influencing the Senate. He was the first native African to rule this expansive empire. According to a few Roman writers, the Black emperor never forgot the imprint of his African birth and early education.

Great pride flowed through Septimius when he was assigned a duty in his native Africa. He headed his legion with pride and professional dispatch.

There were singular accomplishments under Septimius Severus, the general and the emperor. He changed the measurement of miles to leagues. He rebuilt a strategic military camp at Valkenburg which had been destroyed by floods in 42 A.D. Emperor Trajan's engineers rebuilt it in 100 A.D. and Septimius Severus was the last to rebuild it (193-211 A.D.).

Roman coins, which were skillfully made, showed the expression of Severus as being somber. These coins were circulated until the fourth century after Christ.

The energetic, aggressive, and persistent northern tribes in Britain were a constant threat to the Roman fortifications. Rigorous fighting in Britain by trained Roman soldiers could not, at times, contain the supposedly barbaric Caledonians, Brigantes and others. Emperor Hadrian brought his Sixth Legion to York in 122 A.D. in order to quell the disorder. Before his arrival an entire legion, the Ninth, had disappeared completely. Hadrian, while at York, supervised the building of the great wall which bears his name. It stretched from Tyne to Solway. Twenty years later another wall was built to extend to Clyde and Firth. It was named after Emperor Antonius Pius. But the Brigantes pressed the Romans and were subdued.

Into this hostile and stressful atmosphere stepped Emperor Septimius Severus. He was old and ill, and recouping from a campaign against fellow Roman Clodius

Albinus dug in to rebuild the town and camp at York more splendidly than they were before.

During all this work, Septimius died dramatically in 211 A.D. at York in Britain. At the time, he was busy with its rebuilding and fortification against the fiery northern tribes. On his deathbed Septimius is said to have asked his aides, "Is there anything else to attend? Hand it here." His practical attitude toward his own death was admirable, especially when he asked to see the urn in which his ashes would be placed after his death and cremation.

Septimius spoke to the urn and said, "You are about to contain a man for whom the world was too small."

XII
Herodotus Reported On Blacks

Herodotus,the revered Greek Historian, was called by Roman Julius Caesar "The Father of History." Even though this is not true, his view is a sound barometer of respect for this tireless researcher, writer and objective student of man's activities and man's relations to man. It is the profound and objective reporting on Egypt by Herodotus which gives a good glimpse of the real truth about Black participation in ancient world affairs. His uncensored work is a balance to biased and often baseless writings of some European historians who would make the ancient Egyptians Caucasians.

Herodotus reported Ethiopian Menes as the first king of Egypt around 3100 B.C. He was a man with outstanding engineering capabilities. He helped raise the dykes to protect the city of Memphis from the occasional flooding of the Nile River. As to Menes' 30 successors to the Egyptian throne, Herodotus points to 18 Ethiopian kings and one queen, Hatshepsut. To quote the famous Greek, "all the rest were kings and Egyptians."

In his writings, Herodotus calls Black Africans "the handsomest people in the world." He also tells of the Egyptians who consistently conducted health forays into Ethiopia "following the sun."

In an oblique way, Herodotus captured the splendor of Africans when he recounted how he drank wine from brass and bronze goblets. During his visit to Africa, or the Black nations of Africa, he probably saw the custom of guests being served wine before dinner or toasting each other.

One of his outstanding writings explained about the remarkable similarity of the Colchians to the Egyptians. During a massive sweep through Europe by a huge Egyptian army, some of the soldiers were left to control an area on the eastern side of the Black Sea, which is now part of the Soviet Union. Herodotus, more than two thousand years later, compared them with the Egyptians. Their skin was black. Their hair was wooly, like that of the Egyptians and Ethiopians. The Colchians practiced circumcision, which only Egypt and Ethiopia practiced during the period in question. Even more conclusively, Herodotus reported that the Colchians wove their linen the same way as the Egyptians did. This method was not known to any other people. The Colchians, known today by other names, are still in existence in regions also inhabited by the Armenians and Georgian Russians.

XIII
Cush (Ethiopia): A World Power

Ham, one of the sons of Noah, had four sons. They were *Cush*, Miziriam, Phut and Cannaan. Ham colonized an area of North Africa which was designated by the Bible as the *Land of Ham*. *Cush*, the oldest son, pushed his way inland and fathered the *Cushites* whose dark skin color identified them with the people who had colonized Egypt. Ancients have often said that Egypt is Ethiopia's oldest daughter. The Greeks called these people *Ethiops*, or people with burnt faces. *Cush* was located in the Sudan which bordered ancient Ethiopia.

Stephen of Byzantiau, a sixth century dictionary writer, wrote:

Ethiopia was the first established country on earth, and the people were the first, who introduced the worship of the gods and who enacted laws.

Strabo, a first century Greek geographer, says that geometry came to the Greeks from the Ethiopians.

Fabre d'Olivet stated:

The Black race is more ancient than the white, was dominant upon the earth and held the sceptre of science and power. It possessed all Africa and the greater part of Asia.

Ethiopians colonized other nations. Evidence is on monuments in Asia, Arabia and other parts of the world. The monuments show African features such as wooly hair.

Ethiopia and Cush are used interchangeably in the Bible and among some historians. There is no question, however, that Ethiopia was a world power long before other nations, and certainly it was one of the two world powers during the peak of Egypt's greatness. According to Bishop Alfred G. Dunston, Jr. in his book, *The Black Man in the*

Old Testament and Its World, the long held theory about how Ethiopia would "stretch forth her hand" is wrong. Actually, the statement was not one of crying for mercy, reminding nations that fallen Ethiopia would rise again. It was a statement meaning that powerful Ethiopia, with all her greatness, just might have to stretch forth her hand and call on God one day.

The book of Genesis places the original Garden of Eden at Ethiopia stating, *A river went out of Eden to water the garden; and from thence it was parted and became into four heads*. The Bible states further: *And the name of the second river is Gihon; the same it is that compasseth the whole land of Ethiopia*.

During her history, up until this day, Ethiopia put huge armies into the field. They fought the Egyptians, the Assyrians, the Hyksos, the Hittites; and they fought *with* and *for* Israel. The Bible mentions Tirharka, a Black king of Egypt, who came to aid Hezekiah against the Assyrian King Sennacherib.

Since man can remember, Ethiopia, or Cush, carried on commerce with its neighbors and the world. King Solomon of Judea and King Hiram of Tyre sent their ships into Cush to bring back the products of the rich forests and mines. Around 2700 B.C., Africans built flatboats and barges and sold them to Egypt for her sea trade. Ethiopia dealt with Babylon almost three thousand years before Christ. It controlled most of the world's supply of gold, and had skilled goldsmiths who fashioned exquisite jewelry.

The ships of Ethiopia plied the waters of the Red Sea, the Mediterranean Sea and the Indian Ocean. They were made of bullrushes and transported the many products of Cush such as iron, ebony, ivory, elephants and jewelry. It was Job in the Bible who mentioned the "topaz of Ethiopia." Solomon wanted to buy some of the *red gold of Emu*. In the centuries before Christ, the civilized city of Meroe was an artisans center, where iron was smelted and farming tools, cookware and weapons were fashioned. Meroe was also a center of culture. It was the military base from which Piankhy moved his troops against Egypt 800 years before Christ.

Ethiopians were farmers and herdsmen. They taught other nations, including the early Greeks, these techniques of survival.

The association of Ethiopia and Egypt has been constant. It has prevailed from prehistory until today. Some historians and writers claim their findings make it seem like one land. Herodotus, the Greek historian, told of Egyptian expeditions into Cush, or Ethiopia, to find the *Table of the Sun* calendar.

Today there are portraits in Ethiopia of Imhotep, the physician to the king of Egypt twenty-three hundred years before Christ. Imhotep is pictured as Black. Also in Ethiopia today, there are 40 classic paintings of Makeda, Queen of Sheba. There was little question that the Eighteenth Dynasty was comprised of Blacks: including Queen Tiyi, who was a Sudanese; Hatshepsut, the first real Queen of Egypt, who was of mixed heritage; and later, Tutankhamen. But the Twenty-Fifth Dynasty has been generally considered the Nubian or the Black African Dynasty.

Religion has played a deep and significant part in Ethiopia, or Cushite, life. Previously it was stated that the Cushites created many gods which they later passed on to the Greeks. The *one god* theory began in Black Africa and influenced the great Ahknaton, King of Egypt. Yet Ethiopia has held this faith longer than any other nation.

The faith in Ethiopia was grasped with such fervor that there are churches remaining today which were carved out of a single piece of rock. Many churches and temples and other religious monuments were destroyed during the Hundred Years Civil war. It erased some of Ethiopia's most valuable history. It was Egypt who introduced Christianity to Ethiopia in the fourth century after Christ.

Today's Ethiopia makes political use of the ancient line of King Solomon of Judea and Makeda, the Queen of Sheba. It was their son, Menelik, and their relationship which gave this nation its cultural ties with the Jews. This line was forced off the throne in 937 A.D. by the Falashas, or the Black Jewish descendants of Abraham. In 977 A.D. the old line resumed. Haile Selassie was recently deposed and died in prison. He was the modern link with this royal association. He ascended the throne in 1930 and ruled until his death in 1975.

XIV
The Unmatched City of Ancient Meroe

The ancient city of Meroe located in the Sudan has been recognized by true historians as one of the foundation urban communities of civilization. It was African and Cushite based on African soil with an African population. Its existence goes back to pre-history and it grew to vital importance in many areas of life. It grew to be one of the important commodities exchanges. Meroe took its place as a major iron smelting center with which we will deal later. Culturally Meroe was a place where beliefs and diverse thoughts mingled and were expressed.

Early in the Cushite Empire, Napata and Meroe were the chief cities with Napata recognized as the capital. Napata was the sacred city of Piankhy, the Cushite general who captured Egypt and formed the Twenty Fifth Nubian Dynasty. Piankhy's holy city was destroyed by the Romans stationed in Egypt as punishment to Candace of Ethiopia who attacked them. Later Meroe became thc capital city and the "Cradle city."

Considering that Meroe was a multi-faceted city it was principally a center of diverse commerce. It has been compared to the hub of a wheel where the spokes were roads and sea routes leading out in all directions to markets of the world. Where at one time all roads led to Rome, during her heyday, many roads led to Meroe.

This Cushite city on the Nile held enormous deposits of gold and infinite wood sources for fueling the smelting of iron ore. Rainfall was plentiful. Valleys were plush and green for agriculture. The pasturing of animals was idyllic. What did this mother of the iron industry look like? The answers to this question have been contradictory. The city was surrounded by beautiful pyramids and exquisite temples some of which are said to predate those of ancient Egypt. They ringed the city and stood like watchful guards. There are those who say these stone evidences precede the dawn of history itself.

The former second city of the Cushite Empire was politically aware and active. Its relationship to Egypt holds the keys to that part of history which definitely connects great Egypt with the Sudan and the Cushites from the very beginning of Egypt. Meroe watched carefully as Egyptian princes battled to gain personal control of Egypt. In the face of confusion the Governor General of the African-Mediterranean country rebelled. The Cushite Empire stepped in and sent her kings into Egypt, cleared the confusion and set up the historic Twenty-Fifth Nubian Egyptian Dynasty.

Today at ancient Meroe are many granite rams, symbolic of Amon. They lie forgotten in the sand with no semblance of the dynamic religious significance they once commanded.

Discoveries of buried monuments at Meroe have told startling African history. The importance to world history has been shown. Another matter. The sacred pyramids were decorated elaborately with the best form of writing. There were African inscriptions in Cushite and invented handwritings.

Excavators digging at Meroe found evidence of a battle between the Cushites and the Romans. A bronze head of Augustus Caesar was found after nearly two thousand years. This was the battle against Roman legions in bordering Egypt.

African and African-American historians and researchers are obligated in the future to repudiate the distortions imbedded in world history about Africans. There could have been no lack of travel, trade and ingenuity when Meroe had copies of bronze work from China. How did they wear the fine cottons of India?

Omissions notwithstanding a substantial array of facts can be put together. Where Cush had mothered Egypt from the beginning, an ironical twist came about. Pressured Black pharoahs of the Twenty-Second and Twenty-Third dynasties reached down and to the South and gave Cush her independence. Evidence shows that Thutmose I had visited Cush as early as 1525 B. C. Eight hundred years later, Napata held its own religious center for the worship of the sun god Amon. Amon was symbolized by the ram.

In addition to many facts known today about Cush and Ethiopia, there are hundreds of thousands more waiting for historians, archaeologists and anthropologists. Although active research and interest have increased over the last thirty years, before this there was basic carelessness about details of diggings and research. Previously the loss of notes by professional diggers was a cardinal sin, yet some researchers claim they lost notes from Cushite sites.

How ironical it is that present historians, publications and European writers and America still will not admit that:

* Africa has once again become the economic attraction of the world.

* Africa's ancient civilizations are not being ridiculed as loudly.

* Africa's medicines, her practice of medicine, herbs, roots and comedy . . . . since drug manufacturers from all over the world are vying for research positions in Africa.

* Well trained young Africans are overcoming burdensome, oppressive history to rebuild their countries from centuries of European oppression.

During the entire history of Europe, from pre-history to the discovery of America, there was no city or kingdom which could possibly rival Meroe in the ancient and glorious Cushite Empire.

Archaeological investigations in days to come will reveal much which has been lost to history, of a glorious past in Africa . Certainly Meroe qualifies as one of the lost cities of Africa including the extreme vitality of her former existence in trade, culture, many centuries before Christ.

Tragically an ancillary part of ancient Ethiopia, Axum, captured Cushite Meroe and pushed the city into oblivion.

XV
Impact on Asia and the Orient

On the East African coast of the Indian Ocean once lay the Bantu-Islamic civilization of the Swahili. These Africans were trading with India and China many centuries before Columbus was born. In the thirteenth century, the Swahili shipped an elephant to the Emperor's court in China. The ships used by these East Africans were superior to those used by the Europeans during the same period. They were huge, seventy-ton vessels whose structures did not include metal cinchings or nails. Instead they were secured by palm-fiber lashings and were water-tight.

Similar ships left East African Kenyan ports, sailing from Kipini, Mombasa, Kilifi and Kilwa. They made round trips to China and India.

African, Arab and Chinese sailors knew how to plot longitude and latitude at sea. The Chinese knew this technique in 100 B.C., yet Columbus sailed blindly for the New World 1600 years later without this knowledge.

The extensive commerce between East Africa and China uncovered a connection made much earlier between Africa, China and the New World. The Chinese in the thirteenth century recognized the growth and cultivation of maize (corn) in West Africa. Navigators from China told of a New World cereal with long ears. Maize was an American Indian product transferred to Africa through commerce between the Indians of the Western Hemisphere and the Africans who touched America before Columbus.

China, like ancient Africa, had a remarkable civilization before the Golden Age of Greece. The Chinese had early contact with Africa, and their records show that Africans emigrated to China and had economic and social associations with this Far Eastern country. As late as 1935, more than 200,000 Blacks were found living in southern China.

The Swahili states of East Africa completed a significant marketing cycle by handling gold and ivory from the inland countries of Africa and trading them to China, Japan, India and Arabia. In turn, these countries sent back cotton and other useful manufactured goods to the inland people.

Ibn Battuta, a famous world traveler of his day in the thirteenth century, journeyed from the Western Sudan, where Blacks were in power, to India, East Africa and China. He found well-established commerce and centuries-old trade routes.

In Japan the Black man's presence is in strong evidence. The Japanese history books explain the heroism of Sakanouye Tamuramaro. He was a Black who distinguished himself as a general and led the Japanese to victory over the Ainu, a nomadic Asiatic people.

In Japan there are magnificent ancient temples with images of wooly-haired Blacks. This is true in other countries of the East and Far East, where the present inhabitants have straight hair. Among the Japanese, not many centuries ago, Black was considered the color of good fortune.

Sir T. Stanford Raffles has connected oriental habits, ideas, words and traditions with several present day African tribes and with some of the peoples of the South Sea Islands. From the range of the Himalaya, from the Indus to Indo China and on the Malay Peninsula, there are traces of African civilization. The mixed races of the inhabitants are additional evidence.

In the scattered temples of Siam there are idols fashioned exactly like those of West Africans. The same is true in Asia and India. The Hindu idols, Kali, consort of Siva, and Vishnu himself, are represented in a black color.

XVI
Three Black African Popes

Black Victor, a native of Africa, was the fifteenth Pope. He served from 186 A.D. until 197 A.D. during the reign of Emperor Septimius Severus, also an African who had led Roman legions into Britain. Scholars now recognize that it was Victor who reaffirmed the Holy Feast of Easter to be held on Sunday as Pope Pius had done. As a matter of fact, he called Theophilus, Bishop of Alexandria, on the carpet for not doing this. He also added acolytes to the attendance of the clergy.

Black Victor was pope for ten years, two months and ten days. He was crowned with martyrdom and buried in the Vatican next to the body of the Apostle Peter, the first Pope.

Militades occupied the papacy from 311 to 314 A.D., serving four years, seven months and eight days. He decreed that none of the faithful should fast on Sunday or on the fifth day of the week because this was the custom of the pagans. He noted in Rome that there was a Persian-based religion called Manichaenism. The faith of these people called Manichaens who said they could release the spirit from the body through asceticism. Militades decided that consecrated offerings called leaven should be sent throughout the churches with the pope's consecration. It was Militades who led the church to final victory over the Roman Empire. When he died, Militades was buried on the famous Appian Way.

Of the three Black African popes, Gelasius seems to have been the busiest. He occupied the holy papacy four years, eight months and eighteen days (492 A.D. to 496 A.D.). Gelasius followed up Militades' work with the Manichaens. He made an issue of why the Manichaens' gods had not provided calm seas to bring late grain ships to Rome and prevent suffering. He exiled them from Rome and burned their books before the doors of the Basilica of the Holy Mary. He delivered the City of Rome from the perils of famine. As a writer of strong letters to people of all ranks and classes, he denounced Lupercalia, a fertility rite.

The Pope wrote to Femina, a wealthy woman of rank, and asked her to have the lands of St. Peter, which had been taken by the barbarians and the Romans, returned to the church. He told her the lands were needed for the poor who were flocking to Rome.

Today in the library of the Church at Rome there is a twenty-eight chapter document on church administration and discipline. Gelasius addressed it to the Bishops of Lucania, Brittium and Sicily. He also wrote hymns and treaties. In addition, he wrote prefaces to the sacraments and prayers in careful language and many eloquent epistles regarding the faith. In a fiery and bold letter to Emperor Anastasius, he wrote: "There are two powers which for the most part control the world, the sacred authority of the priests and the might of the kings. Of these two, the office of the priests is greater, inasmuch as they must give account to the Lord even for the Kings before divine judgment. You know, therefore, that you are dependent upon their decision and they will not submit to your will." Gelasius was also buried in the Basilica of St. Peter.

Few were amazed that there were Black Popes and Black fathers of the church during the first five centuries. First, because the matter of Black and White had not been fanned to its later hateful pitch. Also, strong Black African countries showed more consideration for Christians and Christianity than other nations did.

Ethiopia was a haven for Christians who were persecuted in other lands. There are records of bishops in Greece and other parts of the world asking asylum for Christians in Ethiopia through intervention from the Bishop of Alexandria and Egypt.

There were Black fathers of the church—men like St. Augustine (the son of a Black African woman) and Cyprian and Tertullian, both of whom were Carthagenians and were black as Hannibal.

Today people are amazed that there were three Black African popes.

XVII
Blacks in the New World

There are numerous documents which tell of the presence of Blacks with Spanish explorers who came to the New World after and with Columbus. Pedro Nino was said to have piloted the ship *Capitania Hispania* on the third voyage.

Blacks were with Pedro de Aviles Menendez when he founded Saint Augustine, Florida, the oldest city in America. Vasco Nunez Balboa, who had Blacks with him, speaks of finding a colony of Blacks in Panama in 1513. He marched across the bottom of the present United States and reached the Pacific Ocean, where Blacks built the first ships in America and planted and harvested the first wheat.

The Conquistadores found Blacks dispersed in small tribes and villages throughout the New World. There were colonies of Blacks in northern Brazil called the Chares. There were others at Saint Vincent on the Gulf of Mexico, where Black Caribs clustered around the mouth of the Orinoco River in present-day Venezuela. There were Blacks among the Yamasee Indians of Florida. In 1775, at the break of the American Revolution, Francisco Garces said he found a race of Black men living side by side with the Zuni Indians of New Mexico. It was his contention that the Blacks had inhabited the area *first*. La Perouse, a French explorer, found Blacks in today's California. He called them Ethiopians.

American Indian legends are numerous about Black men who came from faraway places. According to Peruvian tradition, Black men came and penetrated the Andes mountains. Also in Peru, Blacks were with Francisco Pizarro, who defeated the Incas of Peru and later destroyed them. In his report on *The Third Voyage*, Columbus mentioned he wanted to see the Blacks the Indians told him about.

Seven years before Bishop Las Casas had persuaded the Spanish Crown to allow each settler to bring 12 slaves to America. Balboa claims there were Blacks in the Antilles. This was before any Spanish colony was organized.

Records show there were Blacks with Ponce de Leon and Hernando Cortez. To date, the story of Estevanico, or Little Steven, is the most popular.

Estevanico was among the first Spanish explorers to see Texas, and he was alone when he discovered present day New Mexico and Arizona. He did this 45 years after Columbus touched the shores of the New World. First shipwrecked at Tampa Bay in Florida, Estevanico and his party took eight years to walk along the Gulf and across the northern half of the Mexican territory, almost to the Pacific Ocean. Along with four other men, Estevanico was found almost starved in 1536 in northwestern Mexico. He was then included in an expedition led by Franciscan Friar Marcos de Nizza. The Black man pushed forward, leading 300 Indian bearers in search of the mythical *Seven Cities of Cibola.*

Estevanico was so impatient that his plans went awry. He mistook a pueblo for a sought-after fabled city and ignored the fatal warning of an angry Zuni Indian chief. He and most of his 300 Indian followers were killed on the spot. The few who escaped took the word back to the friar.

The story of Estevanico is still a part of the Zuni folklore.

XVIII
Sunni Ali Ber, King of Songhay

The African kingdoms had been building in West Africa long before Christ. Ghana, great and strong, gave in to Mali. Mali, even greater and stronger, bowed in growth to mighty Songhay. And it was Sunni Ali Ber who brought this mighty African kingdom to the peak of its productive greatness.

Sunni Ali Ber, a leader, fighter and thinker, developed the Kingdom of Songhay into a mighty empire larger than Europe.

Sunni Ali Ber ruled from 1464 to 1492 when Columbus was touching the shores of the New World. He was the first ruler to recognize the true economic and military value of the Niger River and the importance of controlling it. Thus Songhay developed a navy for two purposes: to promote warfare when needed, and to protect the commerce which flowed up and down this magnificent waterway.

In a mighty show of strength, Sunni Ali Ber moved against the Mandingos of the left and right banks of the Niger and brought them under his control. His long 35 year battle was to bring all religions and factions under the control of the Songhay government. His success was quite productive, but not complete. He found it was not enough to favor his own African religion and traditions, while respecting those of the Moslems. Yet, through it all, he accomplished much in the areas of education, agriculture, military organization and trade.

His record stands as having established the largest territorial empire in West Africa, one which surpassed the size of Europe. Before his death, he was about to form an organization called United West Africa.

Sunni Ali Ber, even though African, became a nominal Moslem for the same reason which prompted other Black kings: trade and commerce were in the hands of the Moslems. He was able to build the nation's economy, while developing its people into a unified nation.

This king, who brought his small country to a mighty one, represented strength and traditional African culture. He defended the rights and beliefs of outsiders such as the rites of the traveling nomads and of Moslem scholars of Timbuktu. Also many different languages spoken by people scattered thousands of miles apart were brought together under one nation.

Under Sunni Ali Ber, the vast lands of Songhay were made safe for travelers and merchants. He divided the kingdom into seven districts. Each was headed by a competent governor with his own military complement, advisors and power. This aided Sunni's communications and control.

Even at this point of success, communications and commerce left something to be desired. To alleviate this, Sunni Ali Ber built a navigable canal from Walata to Timbuktu.

Among the many acquisitions for his kingdom, Sunni Ali Ber

added the precious jewel of the city Jenne. He also acquired Timbuktu. Both of these cities operated fine universities whose teachers were both African and Arab. Students came from all over the known world to learn in them.

His name was *Ali*, his dynastic name was *Sunni*, coming from the line of Suliman-Mar. *Ber* means *Great*. Thus, Sunni Ali Ber.

XIX
Great African Warriors

When the centuries old diabolical veil is lifted by Europeans, the glorious black past will come to the fore. General world history, though becoming more balanced and judged anew is not without the censorship of those who wrote with bias They screened away from the world, especially from Africans on the continent and in the diaspora, the greatness of African contributions to mankind from pre-history until today. The screening away knowledge of African history, culture and actual superiority has been criminal to the extent it has destroyed millions of minds and bodies of Africans and their descendants. Also it destroyed the minds and bodies of Europeans who made others feel negatively about themselves in relation to the Africans European and American whites were the historians, journalists, biased writers, publishers . . . even filmmakers who have preached directly and indirectly the supremacy of the white and the inferiority of the black.

The purposeful supremacist writings have destroyed the necessary balance of history, omitting the presence and contributions of Africans, claiming Europeans to be the only producers of anything worthwhile. This includes science, art, literature, military prowess and thought They made the yardstick for measuring the acceptable in world society.

Taking the above as the backdrop, the author walks back through history to refute European superiority on the battlefield. Paraded through these pages will be some of the great military men of all times. And they were Africans.

Ramses III

They came like a mighty swarm of heavily armed locusts. They overran cities in their path They destroyed crops, took cattle, and murdered men, women and children in their wake. They rolled onward like an angry cloud by land and sea. No army or fleet could stop them. These angry men lived on the land as they moved forward. Their supply wagons stretched for miles behind the vanguard of soldiers. The wagons were loaded with the worldly goods of the warriors and also carried their women and children.

They were the Philistines!

No one knew who they were or where they had come from, but on they came out fighting any army or contingent standing in their way.

This menacing horde was first sighted on the coast of ancient Greece. Messengers from villages and scouts from cities carried the word back about the fierce-looking, tall warriors with round shields and bronze swords. The Philistines reached the Mediterranean coast with their powerful fleet which stayed in touch with the army on land.

The moving horde destroyed Sicilian towns and took their prize horses and cattle. At Tarsus they snatched the silver from the famous mines. The Hittites were no match for them. Iron furnaces and their technique for smelting iron was grabbed up by the invaders as they rolled on. The centuries old empire of the Hittites was practically wiped from the earth.

The Island of Cyprus was stormed and invaded while the army crushed its way into Syria. Nothing slowed them down as they sharpened their sights on the prize of the world . . . the nation of Egypt.

But Black Egypt was waiting.

Ramses III was waiting.

Black Ramses III (son of Seti I and grandson of Ramses II) took the whole picture of the invasion into view. He prepared his ships for a skillful defense. He placed his army under the most capable commanders. When the armies met, the power and the anger of the Philistines crumbled under the skill and the tactical organization of the Egyptians. The Philistines were slaughtered. The Egyptians stripped them of their supplies and armor. They took their cattle and horses and claimed the prize stallions they had stolen in Sicilia.

In the battle at sea the gods of the Egyptians were in good form. The wind of the sails on the Philistine boats failed. They were left without power and they could not maneuver. They had to wait for the Egyptian onslaught. On the other hand, the Egyptian boats were powered by humans and oars. They could move in any direction. Craftily they moved within arrows range and showered the enemy. They moved closer and destroyed the crafts, sending them and the soldiers aboard to the bottom of the ocean.

This was 1108 B.C. Although beaten, the Philistines were by no means eliminated. They became an important part of the political life of the known world. They played a key part in the lives of the people of Israel as detailed in the Holy Scriptures.

Tarharka
"The Triple Crown"

Through his numerous military activities, Tarharka became known as "Emperor of the World. " This was a complimentary gesture to the Nubian Twenty-Fifth Egyptian Dynasty and to a singular pharoah of the Black controlled part of world history.

Tarharka was the son of the great Nubian general, an early Egyptian pharoah, Piankhy. Cut from the same military cloth as his father, he has received numerous compliments and complaints from later historians. Sir Wallis Budge, dean of British Egyptologists, said Tarharka offered steadfast resistence to the ever-threatening Assyrians. His opening years as head of the Egyptian empire had two powerful diplomatic and military dimensions: he restored the original power and glory of the Nile Valley

Historian Strabo claimed that Tarharka invaded Europe as far as Gibraltar. His armies were so great and effective that other nations sought non-aggression pacts with him. The nation of Judea sought alliances. Tarharka personally led his Ethiopian army into battle to assist Judean Hezekiah in his bitter fight with the Assyrians. In these fights for Judea, Tarharka destroyed Sennacherib and his Assyrian army. In addition, he recovered the cities of Palestine which had formerly belonged to Egypt. There had been no confirmed historical statements that Tarharka became a prisoner of the Assyrians.

The Bible mentions the strength and mighty skill of Tarharka. In Isaiah 37: 9 the verse states "and he heard say concerning Tarharka King of Ethiopia: He is come forth to make war with thee. And when he heard it, he sent messengers to Hezekiah." Even more descriptive was the reference in Jeremiah 46: 9 "Come up, ye horses; and rage, ye chariots; and let the mighty men come forth, the Ethiopians and the Libyans who handle the shield; and the Libyans, (Black) who handle and bend the bow."

It is noted that some historians admitted to Tarharka's greatness, yet still took a racist blow at him. One English Egyptologist said of Tarharka, "An outstanding epoch of nigger domination."

Hannibal, Black Threat to Rome

No general in world history accomplished so much with so little under such overwhelming odds as Black Hannibal did during the Second Punic War between his native Carthage and mighty Rome in 218-201 B.C. Many centuries later, Napoleon Bonaparte of France was quoted as rating Hannibal above the seven great generals of history. When the records of Hannibal's encounters, victories, strategies and unheard of risks are studied, Napoleon's statement carries indisputable weight. If Black Hannibal, leading a few thousand African troops within earshot of the City of Rome, could evoke the desperate cry from Romans, "Hannibal at the gates," then a deeper look at Hannibal's accomplishments is deserved.

Hannibal was a child of nine when he swore enmity to Rome. This he did at the feet of his militarist father, Hamilcar Barca, for Rome had wrestled the valuable Sicily and Sardinia from his native Carthage in a war which left bitterness and determined vengeance.

Fifteen years later, after maturing war experiences in Spain, Hannibal left Carthage for Rome by an unpredictable and dangerous route. This was in 218 B.C., and young Hannibal faced the tremendous and dangerous task of climbing and crossing the unchartered and winter-gripped Alps mountains. No other route was possible. Roman naval might had blocked him on the water while mountains of northern Italy and powerful Roman armies made his entry into Italy impossible.

With 80,000 men Hannibal began his approach to the Alps, the most costly mountain trip in history. Stopping to let 10,000 men return home, he proceeded into the mountains, commanding men who were speaking scores of languages and many more dialects. The soldiers were Black Africans, Numidians and Spaniards. There were elephants trained in warfare, skilled archers, swordsmen and riders. Most knew little of the kind of winter they faced. In his determined and desperate move across the treacherous mountains, he endured cutting blizzards, huge rock slides and underdog battles with native tribes. The journey cost Hannibal 50,000 men, countless animals and frustrating delays.

The Romans did not hear of Hannibal's plan until much later after his start. Without this knowledge, Rome had planned to invade Africa and attack Carthage with 30,000 men and 160 warships under Titus Sempronius. Another strike force under Publius Cornelius Scipio with 26,000 men was invading Spain to capture long-established Carthage strongholds. Still another force was assigned to Cisalpine Gaul to watch the rebellious Celts, while the major thrusts dealt with Africa and Carthage.

Sempronius heard of Hannibal's unimaginable attempt to reach

Rome over the Alps and marched his army in a parallel route along the Adriatic Mediterranean shore line. Both Hannibal and Sempronius were surprised. The Roman was amazed at the speed with which Hannibal came over the Alps. Hannibal was surprised at being met by a well-equipped and battle-ready Roman army. Hannibal's 20,000 surviving men were weary and ragged but prepared. Hannibal had studied the land area before he confronted Sempronius.

The site was Ticinus.

Hannibal had concealed his elephants and his merciless Black African swordsmen. During his planning, Hannibal had made his center line weak. This is where Romans always hit first and the hardest. Sempronius, apparently encouraged by his superior numbers, charged and struck Hannibal's center with typical Roman might. The Carthaginian line gave and moved slowly backwards with the impact taking the Romans back into a conclave. The armed elephants were turned loose. The Romans panicked, broke ranks and scattered. Thousands were trampled to death by the trained elephants. Amidst the confusion of the Romans, the Black African swordsmen rushed in, slaughtering as they went. Hannibal's first victory had been a disaster for the Romans and word sped to Rome of this tragedy. Fear gripped the land for two reasons. How could an army cross the treacherous Alps? How could so few tired and weary men defeat the army of Consul Sempronius?

This defeat of the Romans by Hannibal was one of many spanning fifteen years, as the Black Carthaginian roamed the Italian countryside foraging and recruiting. His tactics in battle were rarely the same. Hundreds of thousands of Roman legionnaires died at the hands of his smaller forces. At Treba, a month after Ticinus, a small Carthaginian force teased the Roman army to pursue, only to have the Romans bogged down in a marsh and hacked to pieces.

Two Roman armies stood between Hannibal and Rome. Gaius Flaminius had 40,000 men. Gnaeus Servillius had 20,000. Hannibal circumvented them by performing another superhuman feat. He crossed the Apennines mountains. struggled through the impassable Arnus marshes and arrived at the Rome-Arretium Road. He now stood between the Roman armies and Rome itself.

At Lake Trasimine, Flaminius went down before Hannibal, taking 25,000 Romans to their death. Varro and Emilius, co-counsels, with all of 90,000 men, lost one of history's great battles at Cannae, on August 2, 216 B.C. By extending one flank into the Aufidius River and using the weak center tactic again, Hannibal let only 10,000 of the ninety thousand escape. The toll included 80 Roman senators. Battle after battle followed and Romans tasted defeat at Benevertium, Capua, Upper Baetis, Northwest Lucanis and Herdonia. The famous Marcellus was lost at the Battle of Numistro.

Support for Hannibal from his native Carthage was poor, even though he had sent rich proof of his successes in Italy. Also, the Romans were attacking Carthaginian strongholds in Spain and striking and raiding Carthage itself. He was needed there to check the losses being inflicted by the Romans.

Back in Carthage, Hannibal hastened his readiness for battle. He fought his last at the Battle of Zama in 202 B.C. This time his untrained elephants were not effective against Scipio Africanus. The majority of his soldiers were recruits. Most damaging was the help his friend Massinissa gave the Romans with his Numidian forces. Hannibal and Carthage were apparently lost. Severe financial losses and obligations were heaped upon Carthage by Rome and they were met.

Hannibal's ability to rebuild his country was as fine as his generalship. Carthage prospered after the war and his nation was again competing in the world of trade. This displeased the Romans because they felt Hannibal was preparing again for war. Rome decreed that Carthage must be destroyed. It was. Hannibal refused to submit to arrest and fled—first to join Antiochus III, his Syrian friend. Rome pursued him there and Hannibal fled to Bithynia in northwest Asia Minor. Here Hannibal took his own life with poison he kept inside his ring.

Polybius, the Greek historian, had the highest praise for Hannibal. Today the tactics of the wily Carthaginian are still taught at military academies. Though Carthage as a nation has long since disappeared from world affairs, the name of Hannibal lives afterward as proof of the existence of this mighty nation of traders and fighters.

Antar
Warrior and Poet

Antar was one of the greatest pre-Islamic poets of Arabia. He became one of the esteemed poets at the Court of Harun-Al-Rashid. His mother was an Ethiopian slave named Zebbeda. He was born around A. D. 498 His father was a nobleman of Shaddad and was a distinguished member of the Ads, a desert tribe. Antar was a descendant of biblical Ishmael of the patriarch Abraham and his Egyptian wife, Hagar

From a bored, half-starved shepherd boy in a dry, dusty Bedoin village, he rose instantly to leadership among his war-like people. Before the end of his life he had 335 million Moslems shouting his name. In the literature of the East, Antar was called "The father of heroes." It was a long, tumultuous, exciting road from the small village to world power.

Antar achieved greatness in two primary fields as a fearless, conquering warrior and as a writer of breathtaking poetry. For a while they existed apart but later they joined to exalt him more and to leave his mark on the world to praise his unmatched genius in verse and his military prowess as a leader.

As a warrior his career began with the swiftness of lightning. As he tended the sheep in a dry, expansive pasture, the days dragged along; with his lowly station defeating the ambition he might have had. In a war-like village among his people fighting and plundering were a way of life. Antar was not considered at all. Especially he was not regarded as soldier material.

Then it happened.

A neighboring village quarreled with members of Antar's tribe over a horse. Antar was fifteen. One day he heard shouts that the enemy was attacking. Someone thrust a sword into his hands and tossed him onto a horse When the battle was over, Antar had fought so skillfully the village declared him a hero. He was made the official guardian of his people. Gone forever were the dusty field and the grazing sheep. His father, who had completely ignored him before, now acclaimed him and freed him from family bondage.

The horse and the sword took him into many battles, most of which he won. To distant parts of Asia he rode and fought bringing untold jewels and spoils back home to his village and country. One of the driving forces in his life also ultimately brought together his military skills and his writing excellence. The great emotional object of Antar's life was his cousin, Ibla. She was daughter of his wealthy uncle. He wrote about her, dreamed about her, took her name on his lips into battle. When he returned from his conquests in Asia he was challenged by the "invincible" Aboodji for the love of Ibla. The family of his love had been against Antar from the start. But his great wealth and fame had moved all of this aside except Aboodji.

His duel with Aboodji was vigorous and deadly. Antar's experience and tremendous drive prevailed. He crowded Aboodji, rushed him and out parried him. His opponent wearied and dropped his guard. Antar ran him through. Immediately Antar took his bride and her mother and rode away to the wedding.

There is an impressive occasion in which Antar blended war with poetry:

"As soon as I beheld the legions of our enemies advancing cheering one another into battle, I, too, rushed forward and acted without reproach.

"The troops called out, Antar! While javelins long as the cords of a well were forcibly thrust against the chest of my dark steed I ceased not to charge the foe with the neck and breath of my horse until he was mantled in blood.

"My steed bent aside with the staves and lances in his forehead, complained to me with gushing tears and tender sobbing.

"In the midst of the black dust, the horses were rushing with disfiguring countenance from robust stallion and very strong-limbed mare.

"Then my soul was healed and all my anguish was disbursed by the cry of the warriors, 'Well done, Antar Charge again!' "

History has remembered the poetry and the war record of Antar. Seven of his famous poems called "The Mollakat" are on display at Mecca. Rimski-Korsakov's *Symphony Antar* has captured the oriental fire of the great poet's genius. Thirty-two volumes of *Romance of Antar* were published in Cairo. Two editions of the work are "*Syrian Antar*" and "*Arabian Antar*" Where few warriors might have outfought Antar, none compared with him and his genius in the writing of poetry.

Cetewayo

J. A. Rogers, eminent historian and researcher, said of Zulu leader Cetewayo, " His victory against the British at Isaaidlhwana was marked by one of the most terrifying slaughters in the annals of warfare. It finally took England 100 million dollars and her ablest soldiers to cope with this black South African king."

Against the British, during most of his armed struggle, Cetewayo's men wore only a loin cloth. Their armor was a shield of dried hide, two or three spears and a short blade for stabbing. The Zulu warrior could march 30 miles a day. Cetewayo often pushed them to 50.

Cetewayo was the grand nephew of the mighty Shaka. He carried on the expected role of superior military excellence where men met death for neglect of duty. It was when the Boer whites started flagrantly sitting on his land did he move his terrible fighting machine against them.

Like many African nations, Cetewayo's Zulu land had been infested by spying and cheating Christian missionaries. The British, after winning out over the Dutch, began to dismantle Cetewayo's power through punitive laws and regulations. Finally Cetewayo was pushed too far. His resistance ended in the inevitable clash of arms.

The Zulu were known for their excellent physiques and superb strength. Their unmatched daring and their unwavering loyalty to Cetewayo were known everywhere. It was a most prophetic moment for the history of South Africa when the giant warrior said:

"Go back and tell the white men this and let them hear it well. Myself and every one of my men will die first. I give you until sunset to get out of my territory."

The British did not believe Cetewayo. It has been felt that a show of strength of the whites and the African General would give in. Soon 12, 000 British troops invaded his country at three strategic positions. This was in January of 1879. The entire contingent was under the command of Lord Chelmsford and a Colonel Durnfold. They led 11,000 whites and 2,000 black soldiers The British dug in and entrenched themselves behind their wagons. They opened fire with artillery and machine guns. When the chanting Zulu charged, British automatic gunfire cut them down like a lawnmower. Armed only with knives and spears, Cetewayo's men kept up the charge despite the numerous losses. The blacks reached the barricades and jumped from them. Vigorous hand-to-hand fighting ensued much to the grief of the British.

The Zulu killed the entire British army. Approximately 50 escaped downstream of a nearby river by riding their horses into the water. The Zulu killed everything in the British army; the dogs, the horses, and the mules. Dead Africans were piled up in stacks where the machine guns had mowed them down. In a battle of machine guns against spears and knives this costly victory was anything less than miraculous. More than 6,500 British lie in the field. Over 3,500 Zulu lie dead and an untold number were wounded. A prediction of the future was evidenced by the Zulu capture of 40,000 rounds of ammunition with guns.

Cetewayo was on the march. At Rorke's Drift he defeated the British. He scored another victory at Inahalobane. Eventually the British with their superior weapons won out. The great Cetewayo was finally defeated. He was jailed and his country was subdued and occupied.

Lucius Quietus

Black Lucius Quietus was the highest type of Roman field officer. Modern writers have minimized his greatness because of his close association with Roman Emperor Hadrian (117-138 A.D.). Some said he came to the Roman army from Spain. This was no great wonder because black Carthaginians had been in Spain since before the Punic Wars. These conflicts preceded the birth of Christ by two and a half centuries.

Lucius Quietus was, indeed, a friend of Emperor Hadrian with whom he had seen military duty in Dacia. This area is now known as Transylvania and Romania. He was an able soldier from the ground up; an expert with the deadly double-edged Roman sword, the lance and the shield. His superior intelligence attracted ranking officers all the way up to Emperor Hadrian. Lucius had been loyal to Hadrian which was key support to any emperor when exercised by an influential ranking soldier.

The Emperor himself had seen hard military duty in Jerusalem. He was sent by the preceding Emperor, Trajan, to suppress an uprising in Palestine. It was a severe repression historians will admit. It was a Roman military action as was expected. The Emperor had followed the career of Black Lucius Quietus carefully. He had weighed his total capabilities as a soldier and field officer and administrator. It is said he recalled his own stressful experience in Palestine against Bar Kochba and his insurrectionists.

Lucius Quietus was on the cutting edge of significant history. He was sent into Jerusalem. Hadrian ordered it. Titus Vespasianus had attacked Jerusalem in a campaign from A. D. 79 to 81. Now in 139 Black Lucius was to go.

His legions marched into Palestine with banners flying and arms at the ready. As Hadrian had done, Lucius Quietus repeated. He improved on the past. His military feats were adequate. His civilian administration was sufficient. Hadrian was pleased. Soon Lucius Quietus, Black Roman General from Spain, was made Roman Governor General of all Judea. Unmatched historians like Dr. Charles Copher of Atlanta, intimate that Jewish scholars have made their displeasure of Lucius known in their writings of history, literature and even the Holy Bible.

Eighty-year-old General Yusuf Bin Tashfin

Yusef was an eighty-year-old military genius from North Africa, along with his unmixed Senegalese soldiers, who marched into Spain in the 11th century. Yusuf marched to save his fellow Muslims who had been there since 711 A.D. and whose conquests were waning, whose lives were being threatened by the resurgence of Christian power. Yusuf relieved his brothers in Spain on two occasions. The second time he defeated the mighty and popular Rodrigo Diaz de Bevar. In short, it was the indomitable *El Cid.* Names and titles held no meaning for physically fit Yusuf whose intuition in battle was his best weapon.

Yusuf was not born when Yaha, an Almoravid fundamentalist, traveled to Mecca from his home in North Africa to get spiritual direction. His learning developed into a mighty spiritual and fighting force. His sect became the most powerful in Northwest Africa. When Yusuf grew into productive manhood, Abu Bekr was leader of the powerful Almoravidian group. A Moorish work dated 1326 described him thusly:

"Brown in color, middle height, thin, little beard, soft voice, black eyes, straight nose, lock of Mohammed falling on the top of his ear, eyebrows joined, wooly hair." His people lived in the northern border of the Sudan. They were the Masufah

The time had come when Abu Bekr placed Yusuf in command when the leader mounted an expedition to Tunis. Once in command he began to bribe the army with expensive gifts. He took his superior's favorite wife and sat himself in the commander's throne. He built Marrakesh which became the perennial capital of Morocco.

Yusuf was by nature a fighter and a charmer. He extended his empire to stretch from Senegal to the South to the Atlantic Ocean to the west. His command was larger than all of Western Europe.

Another challenge came to him much later in his life. For a century the Moorish descendants of Tarik were losing in Spain. They had invaded Spain in A. D. 711 and had prospered as they took learning, culture, commerce and architecture to this intellectual wasteland. They had defeated the Christians soundly and had established kingdoms in a dozen beautiful cities. Unfortunately Christian Alphonso IV was defeating them at every turn. Capitulation was near when the brothers in Islam called the champion of the faith at Marrakesh, Yusuf ben Tashfin. He was nearly eighty years old. The Moors in Spain needed Yusuf to save their lives.

Yusuf entered Spain with 15,000 men and camels including 6,000 Senegalese. He was welcomed by Moorish kings from Seville, Granada and Almeris. He took command of their troops and is quoted as saying, "Lead us to the enemies of our faith."

The Moors under Yusuf met Alphonso VI at Zalacca in October of 1083. The Christian king had 70, 000 men, outnumbering Yusuf three to one. A field partnership was set up between Yusuf and Motamid of the Moorish kings. It was policy that Yusuf prayed before each battle. Motamid knew the Christians. He did not want to trust them while he prayed. He held the field while Yusuf went to pray. As Motamid expected, the Christians struck. Without the help of mighty Yusuf, Motamid held on, fighting desperately against the experienced Christians. What he did not know was that Yusuf had crossed the mountains behind Alphonso's army and attacked them from the rear. The Moors won the day.

The Moorish kings did not want Yusuf to remain after the victory for fear he would take rulership over them. As promised, Yusuf went back to Africa. Not for long.

Another Spanish Christian leader arose who overshadowed Alphonso IV. He was popular. He was a fighter. He was crafty. He was a winner and he threatened the Moors as had Alphonso. Yusuf marched into Spain again. The combined army met the invincible *El Cid* at Cuenca. The site was a rocky hill surrounded by a small river. This was the battle of battles where Yusuf, his genius and his men, defeated and humiliated *El Cid.*

The builder of Marrakesh had been bothered by the bickering and in-fighting of the Moorish kings in Spain during his first appearance. This time he did not promise to leave. He moved to absorb the Moorish kingdoms of Cordova, Granada, Carmona and Malaga. He extracted huge treasures from each. Before he was through Yusuf was the acknowledged king over 13 kingdoms in Spain and Africa.

Yusuf, the hardy old warrior, lived for 17 years after the battles in Spain. He died as the Sultan of Africa at age 101 in 1108.

XX

Conquerors of Spanish Christians

Yusuf Ben Tashfin was a tall, handsome, commanding figure who never let an opportunity pass to elevate himself. He was second in command to Abu Beher, the leader of the Almoravides in North Africa. Yusuf became the acknowledged builder of Marrakesh, one of the most beautiful cities on the coast of Africa. Through his energy, foresight and leadership, the empire of the Almoravides expanded from African Senegal in the South to the Atlantic Ocean in the West. Tunis and Algeria also fell before him.

In 1080 the Moors found themselves losing ground in Spain. The once-defeated Christians were regaining strength. By strategy they were reclaiming land lost to the North Africans three centuries before. Motamid was the Moslem ruler of Seville. He sent for Yusuf to help him.

Yusuf came with six thousand Black Moslem Sudanese who were the best soldiers anywhere. Of his sixty thousand men, the Blacks were the most skilled and able. Welcomed to Seville by Motamid, Yusuf received the king's ten thousand troops. He combined them with his own soldiers and headed north to battle the Christians—the enemies of his faith.

At the famous battle at Zalacca in 1086, the Christians came in greater numbers wearing heavier armor and maneuvering in an unusually organized manner. In a decision made almost on instinct, and at the right moment, Yusuf called in his Sudanese soldiers and the fight turned into a rout of the Christian knights.

Yusuf was eighty years old at the battle of Zalacca. This did not prevent Motamid from calling on him again when the Spanish had rallied against Motamid behind the formidable Rodrigo Diaz de Vivar, more popularly known as El Cid.

As a renegade mercenary, El Cid had sold his professional army's services to Christians and Moors alike. Ironically he found himself the lone Christian hero of Spain with the exciting threat of meeting the dreaded Yusuf in battle. In 1099 Yusuf defeated the hopeful El Cid and again dashed the hopes of the Christians. Fatefully, El Cid's widow battled the powerful forces of Yusuf, but the Moors and Sudanese finally controlled all of southern Spain.

Ironically a misunderstanding developed between Motamid and octogenarian Yusuf. The old warrior seized Granada, Cordova, Carmona and Madagascar.

He was still king of thirteen European and African countries when he died in 1108 at the age of 101.

XXI
American Black Ancestors

The slave traders and the captors did not snatch their victims from only the bush and the "primitive" villages. Six hundred years ago when the Portuguese explorers invaded the West coast of Africa, they found natives living in well-planned towns with houses and tree-lined streets. There were small populated areas dotted with richly cultivated fields, with flocks grazing on the hillsides. There were remnants of iron furnaces which three centuries before had been used to devise metal implements refined enough to perform eye-cataract surgery.

There were home and village weaving centers where dozens of men and women sat at homemade looms and wove cotton and wool into multi-colored fabrics. Many of these carried designs which had religious, family, historical and occupational significance. At the time of the invasion and capture of some Africans, their local economy, their living standards and the humane quality of their society were superior to that of their captors and certainly more advanced than those of Europe a century before.

To assume that American white slave owners, farmers and businessmen had little knowledge of African capability and background is erroneous. Prospective slave buyers let it be known they wanted a *builder*, or a *good farmer* or a slave who knew about cattle, rice paddies and especially iron-working.

The religious backgrounds of the slaves brought to America were varied. Some had believed in the Black God of Africa for more than a thousand years, in a society where respect for elders was an indisputable way of life and motherhood was sacred. Each man was the father of every child in the village and every child was the son or daughter of every man. They practiced a humanity which precisely defined the Christian ethic of sharing, of caring, of cooperative concern for one another. There were Black Christians among the slaves as well as Black Jews, Moslems and others. There were Moors, Ashanti, Mandingos, Ibos, Fulani, descendants of Alvamorids, and Berbers, but all were reduced to the common bond of slavery. All went through the American system and human wringer and came out *niggers*, *colored* or *negroes*.

The identification with African Blacks and their lives in their homelands was ignored by explorers, slave traders and many European historians and travelers for two main reasons. This knowledge would make the implementation of slavery harder when Blacks learned of their productive past—it would destroy the validity of the excuse of bringing the Africans to America to expose them to Christianity. Finally, there was a great, almost universal bias among writers and researchers. They felt responsible for censoring the African past. Yet the last 150 years have produced concrete proof that hundreds of ruined and abandoned towns and cities remained, to prove the skills and the civilization of those immediate ancestors of the slaves brought to this country.

To point out further the quality of the immediate ancestors of American Blacks we should note their valuable use to the early American economy. European settlers in America in the 15th, 16th and 17th centuries were of the poorer, penniless, less educated and propertyless classes in England, Ireland, Scotland and Wales. They were the prisoners, the jobless and bad debtors. How then could these people know of skilled farming and cattle raising techniques? What could they know of useful and decorative iron-working as seen in Charleston, Savannah and New Orleans? How could they have discovered successful cattle dips, crop rotation and soil revitalization? How could they have known how to build houses, tend rice paddies, and man and control iron furnaces?

Up until a short decade ago, the accepted writings of Europeans and Americans about Black Africans completely ignored all their governments, which prospered at least four centuries after America was discovered, and which never lost their own identity. They ignore those who defended themselves against British armies well into the 19th century. Mainly, the writing and reports were about the broken African peoples who were the victims of famine, mass brutality by other groups and Europeans, and who had surrendered to fate and the elements.

Fortunately today some dedicated Black and white scholars are seeking the truth in West Africa. They are determined to unlock more of the immediate and ancient African past with hopes of giving to the world a new awareness and of dispelling the centuries-old errors and myths which perpetuated the American slave mentality and the slave economy.

PART III

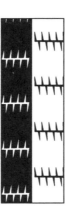

I

A Roman General Died for Christ

Black Roman General Maurice was shaping up his crack infantry legion of 2,000 men when the news came. Emperor Maximian Herculius had ordered him to report with his men to Rome for reassignment. This was nothing new. It was a matter of packing gear in Upper Egypt, sailing up the Nile River into the Mediterranean Sea and on to the port city of Ostia in Rome.

Maurice had been a Christian for some time, and so had most of his African-born officers and men. He had not announced his Christian faith, nor had it ever been in conflict with his duty as a Roman commander.

When he arrived, the Emperor Maximian gave him further orders that did not tell the whole truth. Maurice was told to take his legion to Aganaum (in present-day Switzerland) to put down a rebellion of natives. Immediately after his arrival, a messenger from Rome appeared with new orders. The message from the Emperor commanded Maurice to kill all Christians in the area who had escaped from Africa and Italy.

Maurice assembled his troops, read the orders and declared to them he would not kill his Christian brothers. He was cheered by the men and given full support. The general gave the messenger his refusal to take to the Emperor.

Maximian became furious when he heard the news. He quickly formed an army and marched to Aganaum. Facing Maurice angrily, he demanded that the Christians be killed. Maurice, with his men standing behind him, is said to have replied:

> *We are soldiers, but also servants of Christ. We owe Rome and you military service, but we owe Him homage. We cannot obey you without denying our God.*

Emperor Maximian relieved Maurice of his command and appealed directly to the black soldiers to kill the Christians. When they refused, he ordered every tenth man to step forward. Those men were killed. This was done six times, killing sixty men. Even so, the others stood firm in their faith waiting for death. Offering the soldiers a last chance, the Emperor made generous offers of money and promotions, yet each man stood fast.

Maurice made another statement which has come down through the history of the Catholic Church. He said:

> *We have seen our companions fall under the sword. We have been spattered with their blood. We do not grieve for them. We rather envy them the privilege of dying for the One who dies on the cross for us. Do what you will. No terror or torture can frighten us. We boldly confess that we are Christians and we cannot attack fellow Christians.*

Maximian's soldiers began to hack the Christian soldiers to death. The few that managed to break ranks and flee went back to Africa, or elsewhere in Europe—Germany and Italy. Maurice was killed on the spot.

History has placed Maurice among the other leading Black faithful of the Christian Church, including Athanasius, Clement, Origen, Tertullian, Cyprian and Augustine. In the following century, accounts of the sacrifice were told by Saint Eucherius, Bishop of Lyons. A church was built on the site of Maurice's murder. Later rebuilt by Saint Louis, the patron saint of France in 1264 A.D., the church still stands in the Swiss town of Saint Maurice-en-Valais. Earlier, in 964 A.D., Otto I of Germany selected Maurice as title patron of the Archbishop of Madgeburg. The greatest cathedral there was named after him.

Maurice is still the principal saint of Italy, Spain, Switzerland, parts

During the first, second , third and fourth centuries after Christ, Africans in North Africa fought, bled and died to hold the fragile Christian Church together.

of France and central and southern Germany. Although there has been controversy surrounding Maurice and his position, paintings of him in northern Europe have always shown him as an unmixed black. One of the most famous of these portraits is located near the great organ in the Cathedral at Luzerne, Switzerland.

II

Portuguese Black Royalty

The Portuguese were the earliest traders with Africa. They were the first to find gold for sale and the first to capture Africans as slaves. The country quickly made a monopoly of its profitable position. Along with the lucrative returns from sales, Portugal was introducing African blood into its royal families. This had, and still has, far-reaching effects.

It began in 1441 when Anton Gonsalves brought to Lisbon, Portugal's principal city, a cargo of slaves, along with precious gold from Africa. Later, the traders traveled as far as Nigeria and the Congo. From 1480 to 1530, the Portuguese reaped huge profits on the world market. These were never less than 50 per cent, sometimes they rose as high as 800 per cent. In areas of Portugal, where the wealth grew, the black population exploded. Within two years, 14,000 Africans had been brought in and by the late 1500s, the majority of the inhabitants of the southern provinces were black. In the city of Lisbon, blacks outnumbered whites. it took less than two centuries for the population to show definite African color and facial characteristics.

The royal family became more African than white in appearance. King John IV was not only African in looks, but was said to have come from an illegitimate line. When the wife of the French ambassador, the duchess of Ambrantes, was at the court of King John IV in

1656, she was quoted by writers as saying that the king had the hair, nose, lips and eyes of an African. The royal line is said to have spread to Spain and Italy.

The race mixing of blacks and the Portuguese continued in Brazil. When the Portuguese arrived in 1538, they were already mixed with African. During the early days, the only barrier to marriage was place of birth, not color. The European-born was "superior" to the Brazilian-born. Between 1583 and 1585 more than 15,000 Africans were brought to Brazil. In less than a hundred years blacks became the majority population. The army of black Henri Dios defeated Prince Maurice of Nassau when the Prince tried to help the Dutch move into Brazil. As a result of this struggle, some blacks moved up into the top social class of Brazil which was called Captam-Mor.

A unique situation occurred in Portugal and Brazil. The Jesuits, an established order of the Catholic church, had planned a system of segregation for workers in the mines and plantations which they owned. However, when word reached Portugal, they were warned not to do this.

Because John VI feared Napoleon, he fled with his family to Brazil where he established domain, transferring his throne to that country in 1808. Pedro, the black son of the king, became Emperor of Brazil in 1822. He married the sister of Napoleon's second wife. His daughter, Gloria, became Queen of Portugal. She was a sister-in-law of Victoria, Queen of England.

There are thousands of blacks in America who are of Portuguese descent. Most are identified as blacks. All hold on to their Portuguese names. Individuals from each group have produced distinguished leaders in the general and black communities. The largest settlement in America is in the Bedford, Massachusetts area.

III
Blacks Discovered Europe

It was forty-five thousand years ago when a black people called the Grimaldi discovered the continent now known as Europe. In an unbroken stream of migrations over many centuries they marched north from the Cape in South Africa. On their way, some stopped to settle and develop tribes and nations. Most moved on to settle in Chad, the Sub-Sahara and North Africa.

At that time there was no Straits of Gibraltar and so they walked on dry land into Spain and France. Others walked on land from Africa into Italy, moving northward into Lombardy.

Along the thousands of miles to Europe, the Grimaldi left evidence of their culture such as pendants for ornaments, stone implements for working in the environment and symbols of communication. They also left musical instruments and the first bow and arrow. After they reached Europe, they dispersed into Bulgaria, Switzerland, Illyria and southern Europe on the Adriatic Sea and in Brittany. The last, Brittany, is today's England, Wales, and Scotland.

How did these black Grimaldi look? Their noses were very large and flat at the base. Their facial and head characteristics resembled the Koramus people of South Africa and the Bushmen who were to come many thousands of years later. They have been compared in appearance to modern blacks. Some wore their hair in styles that resemble today's cornrows, that is plaits arranged in parallel lines across the head. Others wore a style also similar to today's peppercorns, when the hair is put into little black rolls or beads. In another style, they fastened their hair into short, close-growing clusters.

These blacks were accomplished and cultured, bringing with them arts and survival skills that gave a new life to the stale and stagnant Neanderthal period in Europe. during the later Paleolithic period, the Grimaldi were the most powerful and influential force on the continent.

The Grimaldi contributed greatly to the early or first arts of Europe.

Their statuettes uncovered by archaeologists reveal extraordinary workmanship. They are definitely the oldest sculpture created by man. The statue of the "Maid of Willendorf," found in Austria, has been called by Graham Clarke, writing in the *Dawn of Civilization*, "the first signs of art on earth." These meaningful discoveries also show the extent of their migration. Pieces of Grimaldi sculpture have been found in southern Siberia and Russia.

However, touring exhibits of "Ice Age Art" from Europe do not make any mention of the art of the Grimaldi. No explanation for this has been offered.

The Grimaldi disappeared! Where did they go? The authorities on pre-historic Europe and pre-historic peoples have no sound answers. It may be that some historians vigorously tried to promote the non-black Cro-Magnon over the Grimaldi; even though the Cro-Magnons came much later and could be descendants of the Grimaldi.

The Grimaldi disappeared around 12,000 B.C. There are several theories offered as to why this occurred. One claims that the Cro-Magnons exterminated them. Another suggests intermarriage, or race mixing causing the Grimaldi to lose their black color. Still another infers that the Grimaldi moved to other parts of the world, mixed with other peoples, and became other nations.

Nevertheless, diggings on the European continent are evidence the Grimaldi were its earliest inhabitants. The opening of Grimaldi graves and other excavations have revealed skeletons and artifacts in layers *below* those of the Cro-Magnons.

The Grimaldi left the bow and arrow and other useful tools. These artifacts enabled thousands of generations of barbaric people of Europe to survive through pre-history until the coming of the Romans.

IV
Two Blacks Fought Over Rome

It has been documented that in 193 A.D., a distinguished black Roman general named Septimius Severus became the emperor of mighty Rome. Further research reveals that Severus was not Rome's first black emperor. What is more, he was forced to fight another black, a Roman general named Pescennius Niger, for his right to rule the empire.

Two black Africans, Helvius Pertinax and Didius Julianus also held the emperor's seat in 193 A.D. After Pertinax died on March 28, 193 A.D., three generals contended for the throne in a fierce and deadly fight. They were Clodius Albinus, who was white and Niger and Septimius who were black. All three commanded large, powerful Roman armies in separate parts of the empire. During those times, Roman generals could play crafty politics with the support of their armies. Julius Caesar did this as did many others.

Niger, whose name identified Africans during this period, was in Syria at the time the fight for the throne began. The people of Rome called for Niger to come home and restore peace. Clodius Albinus was in Britain with his army while Severus was in Pannonia (an area that is now Hungary and Yugoslavia.) Of the three contenders, Severus was probably the first to tell his troops about the possibility of being elevated to emperor by the Roman Senate. They gave him their support, promising to fight and win over the other two Roman armies.

In a shrewdly written letter to Clodius in Britain, Severus promised Clodius the title and position of "Caesar." This pleased Clodius and made him feel that Severus was his friend. It also kept Clodius quiet while Severus planned war with black Niger.

Severus decided to march on Rome first. When he arrived, his reputation as a superb fighter and excellent general caused a panic in Rome. Once there, Severus found that it was not too difficult for the Senate to declare him Emperor of Rome. However, this was just the beginning. He would have to deal with Clodius and Niger.

When black General Niger learned about Severus' elevation in Rome and the new emperor's plan to march against him, he hurriedly prepared defenses in his regions in Syria. His governors, likewise, built defenses in their provinces. The narrow passages and the cliffs of the Taurus Mountains were guarded carefully. The famous and rich city of Byzantium, with all its strengths, was especially fortified. This was to be the point that would block Severus from crossing into Asia from the modern Dardanelles.

In order to make time, Severus subjected his troops to a grueling forced march along the sea of Marma (now called Kapu Dagh). He defeated Niger's first army at Cyzicus and then swept through several other cities. In a final attempt to save himself, Niger recruited hundreds of young men from Antioch, trained them while on the march, and faced his black African brother at Issus. This spot was near ancient Iskenderun in Turkey, the place where Alexander the Great had defeated the Persians almost five hundred years before. A sudden, turbulent storm played a decisive role in this battle—as storms have done throughout history. The driving rains were at Severus' back giving him the advantage, while the wind and the rain were in the faces of Niger's troops. Niger lost. After Severus captured Antioch, he ruled Rome until his death in 211 A.D.

V
The Brightness of Dark Africa

European explorers, historians and contemporary writers found it necessary to call Africa "dark." Others have described it as "The Dark Continent" and "Mysterious Africa." These connotations have had harmful effects on the minds of people, especially blacks, who feel that Africa is not acceptable or desirable in their lives and education. When the Europeans entered Africa at the outset of the sixteenth century, many of Africa's achievements had already taken place, beginning with ancient times and up to this period. The greatness that remained was in the flourishing African kingdom of Songhay, which did not decline until America was discovered.

To refute the claim of African darkness, there are hundreds of facts. The first civilization was developed in the Nile Valley. Iron was first smelted, gold was discovered and refined, the first family was structured and the first formal religion was created—all in Africa. The blow gun, whose principle was later improved upon with the invention of the rifle, machine gun and rocket, was discovered in Africa. The first stringed instruments for music were made in Africa as were bagpipes and the attendant bellows which were used also for fires and other chores.

The science of making dyes, of mixing paints and colors, of printing colors and patterns on cloth and glass, the first techniques of agriculture, the marriage institution, the formation of laws and government were all African in origin.

In East Africa, above the Losidak Range, stands an observatory more than 2,500 years old. Modern astronomers say there was a direct relationship which tied the observatory in with the 365-day calendar year. It matched the year-length calendar of the ancient Cushites. Also in East Africa there are the remains of forced draft furnaces which made a medium carbon steel over 2,000 years ago. This steel was not reproduced until the last century in Germany.

Within the last 800 years, Africans practiced the lost art of sand molding. They poured molten metal into a mold dug in the sand. The liquid metal did not seep into the sand, nor did the sand cling to the metal.

From the 9th to the 14th centuries, East Africans used the ports of Kilwa and Mombasa (now Kenya) to great advantage. They traded with China, Japan, Asia and Arabia. Gold, silver, rugs, teakwood, cotton and ornaments made in foreign countries were exchanged in their market places. East Africans did business with black merchants in the landlocked interior of the country. They relayed their goods to the world markets and brought back the goods that central Africans wanted from China, Japan and Arabia.

While Europe was fighting its way out of the Dark Ages, the Lake Region of Africa was alive with culture and prosperity of the kingdoms of Ghana, Mali and Songhay. Universities flourished, African students learned art, music, law, medicine, architecture, engineering and philosophy. Farmers grew sufficient produce to send caravans to North Africa. Goldsmiths and iron workers proudly performed their tasks, with their families boasting of specialists in these crafts going back ten generations.

When Spanish explorers in the new World found Indians with gold tipped African spears, they took the spears back to Spain and analyzed the gold. It was eight parts gold, eight parts silver and six parts copper. The Spanish realized that this was the same alloy made by the people of Guinea in West Africa.

From the beginning of the Christian Church, blacks in North Africa fought and died to keep it alive. From the time of Christ, until 415 A.D., black men such as Saint Cyprian, Saint Augustine and Tertullian headed the church and helped hold it together. Through Africans, the Christian Church was introduced to other parts of the world.

During the height of the Christian persecutions in Rome and throughout the Empire, healthy wild animals were imported for the sporting games in Roman cities and provinces. For trained African hunters and businessmen, this was a lucrative trade and they handled it well.

Ethiopia was, and still is, the oldest government in the world.

All known literature, since man began to write, has recognized Ethiopia. This includes Greek mythology, the Bible, and all others—until European writers felt it necessary to play down the achievements of blacks.

Until this century, the African medicine man was laughed at by Americans and Europeans. He was seen as a comedian while treating the ill with herbs, roots, branches, leaves and potions. Today some of the world's leading drug manufacturers are in Africa competing with each other to develop some of these same roots, herbs, leaves and potions for the world market.

Little credit has been given to the African for his knowledge of physics and chemistry, and yet there are buildings in Zimbabwe structured so that the weight of the water below supports the weight of the building. Even though they were built more than 1,500 years ago, some are still standing.

Africans brought to America as slaves were weavers, farmers, builders, herdsmen, iron workers. They were not the bumbling people described in British and American literature and records.

Instances of African originality could fill hundreds of volumes. Seeing the evidence listed above shows how unfair it is to call Africa "the dark continent."

VI
Black Caesar Murdered

Pertinax, a Black man, was first recognized as a brilliant student at the University of Carthage. He was taught by the famous Appollanaris, whose students gained world fame. As the Emperor of Rome, Pertinax became the most famous of all. Using his brilliance and his unusual grasp of reality, he worked his way upward, beginning as a small dealer in charcoal in his little North African home town to become the holder of the highest office in the world.

Long before he became emperor, Pertinax qualified as an outstanding teacher. After the retirement of Appollanaris, Pertinax replaced him at the University of Carthage. However, the job did not pay well and so he joined the Roman Army.

As a soldier, Pertinax had a spectacular career. His alertness, bravery and exceptional administrative ability gained him one promotion after another. Within a few years, he had become proconsul of Africa, the equivalent of today's lieutenant general. Having received both an education and military training, he was put in command of a full Roman Legion, with responsibility for thousands of civilians as well. Because of his splendid record, he was chosen emperor of Rome by acclamation.

The shortness of Emperor Pertinax's reign may have been due to his honesty and desire for good government. One historian said of his 87-day term that "He ruled his subjects with wisdom and benevolence." These qualities, however, were not enough. There was still the deadly politics of Rome.

Shady deals, involving buying and selling of government property, were rampant. The preceding government of Commodus had left its legacy of illegal operations. Worst of all, corruption had spread throughout the Roman Army. When Pertinax moved to correct these unlawful operations, which were a heavy drain on the Roman treasury, he underestimated the tremendous political power of the armed Praetorian Guard. At times, this private military unit had even overruled the will of the Roman Senate.

In broad daylight, as he moved through the halls of the Senate one day, some of the Praetorian guards rushed him. In the same manner as the great Julius Caesar was struck down, Emperor Pertinax was punctured with a dozen knives.

Few Roman emperors enjoyed the favorable reports of so many historians. His African birth was openly noted. There was little reason to hide it for at that time Blacks held high offices in the military and provisional governments throughout the Roman Empire. By coincidence, the emperor to follow him was also Black. He was Septimius Severus.

Some of the praises of Pertinax read like poetry. One writer said, "He adorned the throne of the Caesars with the nobility of a true Roman." He was honored for "patriotic conduct and a blameless career." Historian Don Cassius wrote, "A golden statue was erected to the honor of Pertinax in the Circus Maximus as a permanent testimony of public esteem." Throughout his native North Africa, especially in his birthplace at Hadrumetum, there were stone tablets citing his greatness as emperor and caesar. One still stands at Sba-Meghata on the banks of the El-Kantara River. His most impressive tribute is an altar built by African colonists of Rome in one of his former districts. The inscription reads: "Pertinax, Emperor and Caesar."

VII
Mother of Saint Augustine

Monica, above all, was a strong African woman. She loved Africa and she loved her God. She was born in a Christian home in Tagaste in North Africa. The city was under the control of Black Carthage.

Very few women in Christian history have been praised and remembered the way Monica has. She was the mother of Saint Augustine. She lived a moderate and fruitful life. Her people were one of the oldest black peoples of Africa. She recalled many times how she had been raised by a faithful slave. Her memory was always clear and dear of an aged servant who had been in her family long enough to have carried her grandfather in his arms.

Monica was eighteen at the time that she married Patricius. He was a typical North African non-Christian. Schooled by the hard and varied experience of Roman army service, he resisted her constant, mild, yet forceful urging to convert. For many years they coexisted with different faiths until he was finally converted. Monica's urgings prevailed.

Her first born son was Navigus. The second child, a girl whose name was not recorded, is reported by Augustine to have served the church as a nun. The name and life's activity of Monica's third child, also a girl, have been lost to history. The great Augustine, whose birth name was Aurelius Augustinius was her last and second son.

Early in his life, Monica saw in Augustine a special talent for leadership in the Christian Church. She pursued it being a typical African lioness who fought for her cub against outside harm. At the same time she fought him for his own salvation. Her insistence was aggressive and unwavering. He *had* to give his life to the church.

According to Augustine, his mother became both sign and symbol of the dutiful and faithful Christian who—with infinite tolerance—never gave up or failed to be loving. To him, she was almost too good to be true. Probably this was his way, his polite way, of saying Monica dogged his tracks. She never let him rest! She preached and lectured, cajoled and even harassed him; from his pre-student days at home, to his college days at the University at Carthage and to his professorship at the University at Milan, Italy.

Monica had a dutiful obsession. She would turn her son away from his life of intellectual paganism, drinking and loose associations with women. She urged him to end his common-law relations of twelve years with an African girl by whom he had a son.

Monica was determined that his brilliance, scholarship and leadership potential would benefit the Christian Church. In 385 A.D., she took a spring trip to Milan and moved in with her son. Augustine was then a teacher and head of an African colony in the city. He described later his mother's dynamic personality at that time. He told how she had a calming influence on the crew and passengers during the stormy passage from Africa to Milan.

Through her flawless determination, her goal became a reality. In Milan she won the friendship of Ambrose, the Bishop of Milan. He helped her urge Augustine to join the Christian Church. When her son was baptized by Ambrose in 387 A.D., she was relieved and overjoyed.

Failing health did not diminish Monica's joy. While in Milan, she offered her service to the church as she had done in Africa. She had another deep-rooted wish, or prayer. This stayed with her as she started her trip back to her beloved Africa, where she wanted to be buried. She prayed that her son would remember her at the altar of God.

Monica had no dream of his becoming a Bishop of Hippo in North Africa or of his making lasting contributions in his writings and teachings. These contributions have been accepted by major Christian denominations for the last 1,700 years.

VIII
A Deeper Look at Aesop

In the first part of this book the author states that Aesop, the great story teller from ancient times, was black. Aesop was a Simian slave who was sold on an auction block in Asia Minor five centuries before Christ.

The Ethiopian created more than 300 fables, all of which have come down to us from 2,600 years ago. Although many of them are said today to be written by other authors, the touch and style of Aesop remain evident. All have a lesson for life. *The Goose and the Golden Egg*, for instance, teaches about greed. A man finds that his goose has laid a golden egg. Instead of waiting for more golden eggs on a daily basis, he kills the goose to get all of them at once. He opens her up only to find *no* eggs.

Belling the Cat is better known to Americans as *Who's Going to Bell the Cat?* There was a group of mice who lived in stark fear of the cat in the house. After a very serious meeting, they decided that if a bell were put around the cat's neck they would always know his whereabouts. The big question was which one of the mice would put the bell around the cat's neck?

In Aesop's tale about *The Dog and The Shadow*, a dog with a piece of meat in his mouth walks across a narrow bridge. Looking down into the water he sees his reflection. Thinking this is another dog with another piece of meat, he drops his own piece to take the piece from the reflection in the water.

Aesop's genius led him to use animals in his fables. Readers of Aesop can recognize everyday expressions taken from his fables. The expression "sour grapes," for instance from *The Fox and The Grapes*, is very famous.

A fox wanted some juicy grapes to quench his thirst. Coming to an arbor loaded with juicy grapes, he jumped up to grab a bunch of the grapes and missed. Again he jumped and missed. After several more failures, the fox walked away with his nose in the air. "I am sure they are sour," he concludes. In many of Aesop's other fables his animals also teach men lessons in honesty, fear, reason and justice. Among these are *The Wolf in Sheep's Clothing, The Town Mouse and the Country Mouse* and *The Hare and The Frogs*.

Down through the years, Aesop's fables were used for many purposes. During the Tyrannical Epochs in Greece when free speech was dangerous, his fables were used for political purposes. When democracy returned, the Greeks continued to tell them.

More than 200 fables by Aesop were collected in the Library of Alexandria in Egypt. A man named Phaedrus of Greece was also responsible for putting a great number of them together. Centuries later in India, the Buddha Sakyamun used the fables for morale purposes. Around 241 B.C., people in ancient Ceylon read and enjoyed them. As late as 229 A.D., Roman Emperor Marcus Aurelius had a small collection of them, then called "Libyan Fables." Aesop's tales spread into North Africa where the son of Roman General Alexander Severus studied them.

Aesop's fables became part of the intellectual world of Europe during the Middle Ages. Those collected by Phaedrus centuries earlier were prize reading as late as 1030 A.D. During the twelfth century, England developed what they called a home for Aesop's fables. In the thirteenth century, Marie de France translated them into French and in 1484 William Caxton made the first English translations. These were followed by translations into Dutch, Italian and Spanish. Eventually the fables were used as the basis for reading and spelling books. Now they are a part of modern folklore.

In these simple, short and direct stories which place animals in human roles, Aesop displayed a wide knowledge of life and the human condition. His fables have been used as teaching tools for the young and the elderly in a hundred or more languages and dialects.

One of the most lasting of Aesop's fables, called *The Fisher*, has strong political and historical overtones. It has been read, used and enjoyed in many nations. A fisherman took his bagpipe to the river and played for hours, but no fish jumped from the river into his net. He put away the bagpipe and cast his net into the water. Soon he hauled in a net full of struggling fish. The fisherman played his bagpipe again and the fish began to dance. The message in this fable is clear: "When you are in a man's power, you must do as he bids you."

IX
Sophonisba: A Beautiful Black Sacrifice

The love for Sophonisba by two powerful rulers had a tragic ending. Around 213 B.C., the Second Punic War between Rome and black Carthage was coming to a furious and bloody end. The results of the classic struggle were many. Two black nations, Carthage and Numidia, were pitted against each other. Numidia was divided. Rome was shakily re-established as the most powerful nation on earth. It brought about a world-famous love triangle.

Some of the world's greatest poets and dramatists later wrote about Sophonisba. The Carthaginian princess has been compared to Cleopatra, Queen of Egypt, who lived 200 years later.

In 1515 the Italian playwright Gian Giorgio Trissino wrote *Sophonisba*, the very *first* Italian drama. Between 1776 and 1779, Italian Count Vittorio Alfieri wrote 19 tragedies. Among them was *Sophonisba*. The Carthaginian beauty was also the subject of plays by French playwright and philosopher Voltaire and French dramatists Pierre Corneille.

The main character in this real political world tragedy was Sophonisba. She was the niece of the great Carthaginian general, Hannibal, and the daughter of his brother, Hasdrubal. In 213 B.C. Hannibal was away in Italy slowly bringing the Roman Empire to its knees. Rome had only one choice. It was to attack Carthage, Hannibal's homeland and sack Carthaginian towns and cities in Spain.

Syphax was a dashing, intelligent, young king who ruled over

Sophonisba—Carthaginian princess, niece of Hannibal the Great.

one part of black Numidia. The other part was ruled by Gala, whose strong and promising young son was named Massinissa. Sophonisba's father, Hasdrubal, although he was a Carthaginian, admired Massinissa very much. He gave his daughter Sophonisba to Massinissa, who was at this time headed for Spain for advanced military training.

For some unknown reason, Syphax attacked Carthage. The Romans, who were already embroiled with Carthage, were inspired by this move. They asked Syphax to aid them against Carthage. In return, the all powerful Rome would grant his every wish.

When the Carthaginians heard of Syphax's secret deal with Rome, they rushed to Gala, the second Numidian king, for help. In order to counter Syphax's move and prevent his aiding Rome, the Carthaginians gave Sophonisba to Syphax as his wife. This was done without the knowledge of her husband, Massinissa, or her father, Hasdrubal. When Massinissa came home to Numidia after his father's death, he was chased out of the country by rival political forces. He returned to Spain, joining the Roman side against Carthage.

Syphax who was now fighting for Carthage and his wife, had to defend the country against both Publius Scipio of Rome and Massinissa. The Carthaginians lost desperately. Syphax was about to give up when 4,000 troops arrived from Spain and came to his aid. Sophonisba appeared before him and begged him to continue to fight and save Carthage. Syphax tried and failed again. This time he was captured. He told the Roman general that he had broken his alliance with Rome because he loved Sophonisba. He was sent as a prisoner to Rome where he died.

After the final battle, Massinissa, who had been victorious, met Sophonisba again. She told him of how the Carthaginians had desperately traded her for the country's survival. Although he believed her and forgave her, Massinissa would not break his pledge to Rome. He sent a message to Sophonisba along with a potion of poison. In a moving note he told her that because of the political situation, he had no power over his fate. It would be impossible for him to fulfill his duty as a husband to her. He offered her the choice of going to Rome as a prisoner or taking her own life. Her reply to him was as follows:

I accept this wedding present. Nor is it an unwelcome one, if my husband can render me no better service. I would have died with greater satisfaction had I not married so close to my death.

After the war ended, Rome made Massinissa king of all Numidia. Probably Leonard Cottrell summed it up best. In his book, Enemy of Rome, he said, "For the first time in this long and bloody war, Aphrodite, the goddess of love, entered the conflict and her power proved greater than that of many armies."

X

Julius Caesar Wept for Carthage

Due to the military genius of black Hannibal of Carthage, mighty Rome suffered tremendous human and material losses. Its humiliation at being thrown into a national panic would not be easily forgotten. Hannibal had invaded Italy. He moved about at will, destroying one Roman army after another. He came within view of the gates of Rome itself. The only flaw in his campaign was the lack of support from home.

Rome offered military assistance and riches to a Numidian king, Massanissa. He helped the Romans defeat Hannibal and Carthage. It was after the utter defeat by the Romans at the battle at Zama in 202 B.C. that the great black nation saw its end. Even though Carthage paid Rome her required damages and rebuilt her cities and her kingdom, Rome feared the black empire would threaten her might again.

The Roman Senate, under the influence of powerful Senator Marcus Cato, or Cato the Elder, decided that Carthage must be destroyed. This became a rallying cry throughout Rome as each citizen greeted each other with the words, "Carthage must be destroyed." The Romans made their final move during the Third Punic War (149 to 146 B.C.) and attacked Carthage, leveling it to the ground.

More than 200 years later, Julius Caesar grieved over the cruelty of his ancestors' vengeance. He had secretly admired the military genius of Hannibal and superb industry of the black nation. Black historian J.C. DeGraft Johnson in his book *African Glory*, said that when Caesar was encamped near the ruins of Carthage, he had a dream. There were armies of men crying and screaming in misery. After this Caesar promised to rebuild Carthage. Before he could begin, he was assassinated.

Caesar's successor and stepson, Caesar Augustus, carried out the plan, even though many Romans considered Carthage a cursed city. Under the most organized discipline, Augustus rebuilt it again to its African beauty, this time in the finest Roman architectural style. There were theatres, palaces, gardens, baths, forums and market places. The Romans also built a splendid road to connect Utica and Carthage. The beautifully groomed suburbs called Megara were restored.

For a second time Carthage had been raised from the dust. Again she became a powerful world center. In education, Carthage rivaled her benefactor, Rome. The universities of Carthage gave brilliant scholars to the world. Some of these men became fathers of the early Christian Church. Carthage became the leading site of the Christian Church in opposition to Rome. Caesar had been dead for four centuries before peace was made again between Carthage, the Church, and Rome.

XI
Black Sahara: 8,000 Years Ago

Some of the world's most respected historians contend that the first organized society of humans lived 8,000 years ago, about 6,000 years before Christ. Recent discoveries disprove this in favor of the existence of earlier black societies. There were black people living together in a productive situation 6,000 years before Christ in the Sahara region of Africa.

The Sahara region was not a desert then, but a lush, green and fertile land. The people farmed grain and other things to eat. They raised cattle for milk and food, using rawhide for shelter and clothing. They were a sensitive and thinking people who produced a simple art describing the level of their civilization.

These people lived off both domesticated and wild animals. Among them were spotted wild oxen, loping rabbits and giraffes. Horses and camels came centuries later. Drawings found on the walls of their caves show cows tethered and standing peacefully to be milked. Water for cooking, drinking and washing was dipped from wells with leather buckets.

They observed a distinct division of labor. The women performed certain chores; the men did others. It was the men's job to split firewood with axes. They trained, hunted and fought with bows, arrows and spears. They created their own law enforcement and judicial systems. Wall paintings show judges seated on a raised bench. Before them a man stands, guarded by two officers of the court. Another scene shows a man already sentenced being taken away.

As in other African societies, life was shaped by the extended-type family. Everybody owned all the land, the cattle, the flock, the grain and the products. Every person cared for every other.

Women played a more important part in this community than they did 4,000 years later in the same area. They cooked in clay pots, which meant they had a sound knowledge of pottery making. They tended cattle, raised children, gathered food in the field and fashioned

When the Sahara was fertile, Africans raised cattle, dug wells and provided themselves with water, 6,000 years before Christ.

jewelry such as necklaces and bracelets. They made baskets and other items for household and personal use.

As farmers, these industrious people passed down through history an item that has been used in hundreds of African societies since 6,000 B.C., the digging stick. It was used for tilling the soil and getting to edible roots in the ground. Today this tool is still used in African and non-African communities.

They danced for religious and artistic purposes. The men wore richly decorated leggins and chalk-like masks. The women wore colorful ribbons in their hair.

During periods of relaxation both men and women played a stringed instrument that looked like a small version of today's harp. They also played flutes. Probably they took part in group singing.

The life-style of these blacks in the Sahara had a strong impact upon civilization. They lived in an organized, self-help, productive, harmonious community 2,500 years before Egypt was heard of; even before Egypt became a fledgling civilization. When the Greeks, then later the Romans, came onto the world scene these blacks had been in a civilized setting for 5,500 years.

XII
Hypatia: Black, Beautiful and Brainy

By any standards during any age, the stately black Hypatia was beautiful. However, while her beauty may have been an asset, her brilliance and her great flair for speaking were her downfall.

Around 400 A.D. Hypatia lived in the great, teeming and historic city of Alexandria, Egypt. She had a reputation as a spell-binding speaker and influential teacher that was felt throughout all of Egypt and beyond. Hypatia was a philosopher and a mathematician. She used her intellect to charm the multitude—in a profitable way.

The chariots of the wealthy crowded the street outside her academy in the beautiful section of classic Alexandria, the memorable city of Cleopatra. Her writings were read extensively. However, her writings and fame were lost, only to be revived years after her savage murder.

Hypatia's murder was directed by Saint Cyril, Bishop of the Diocese of Alexandria and Doctor of the Church. St. Cyril, a powerful force in the church, was distinguished for his hatred of heretics and heathens. He was also the legate to Pope Celestine. St. Cyril resented a close relationship Hypatia enjoyed with a man the Bishop disliked.

While walking toward her academy one afternoon, a band of monks, servants of St. Cyril, followed her. Once inside the building they attacked her with clubs. She was killed instantly.

It is not clear which of Hypatia's teachings were in conflict with the Christian Church. Was it the famed Nestorianism which Cyril fought so vigorously? There are no records available which show if Cyril's deed was ever criticized by the church.

XIII

White Slaves, Black Masters

Ironically mass white enslavement in Europe and Africa preceded black slavery in America by 700 years. In various brutal military operations, Arabs and Africans snatched two million whites from Europe long before Columbus sailed westward, many years before the first black slaves were brought from Spain to Central America in 1505.

The Moors of North Africa of the sixth century were the direct descendants of the mighty ancient Carthaginians. By 711, the Moors had become a powerful political and military force in North Africa. Summoning the strength of the Senegalese to the south, they built one of the most powerful military machines the world had ever seen.

Under Tarik-bin-Zaid, they rolled into Spain. The German Visigoths fell before them. Moving northward into France, the Christians were soundly defeated at the city of Tours. At the same time in Eastern Europe, the African-Arab combine was overrunning Sicily and sacking the Vatican in Rome.

For the first time in recorded history, a non-white people were dominant in Europe. As conquerors have done since time began, the Africans began an enormous traffic in slaves.

As always slavery was a lucrative business. Other adventurers and nationalities joined in to make money from the conquerors. Private companies and powerful individuals took part. From far away Holland, Sweden and Finland, slaves were brought. The trade reached out to Greece and southern Russia. The conflict raged in Spain for seven centuries where the Africans ruled that country until the twelfth century. Thousands of Spaniards were sold into slavery in Africa and the Middle East. Military campaigns in connection with slave trading began with the successful conquests of Tarik-bin-Zaid in 711 and continued until the victories of Yakof Al Mansur in the twelfth century.

The slavery practiced in Africa and the Middle East was far more humane than that conducted five centuries later by European and American Christians. In Africa and the Middle East the captors dealt with slaves according to a merit system. The more talent and skills the slave possessed, the more easily he could gain his freedom and the faster he could improve his overall social condition.

The system of slavery practiced by the Africans and Arabs also answered a critical need for labor for new building programs, more domestic help and, above all, personnel for the military. Educated captives were quickly groomed for government posts where, in many instances, the efficiency was low.

Arabs and Africans did not base slavery on race and color, as the Christians did later. The era of race prejudice had not come.

Enslavement resulted from lost battles or kidnappings. After arriving in Moslem-controlled Africa or the Middle East, slaves often won freedom by accepting the religion of their captors and saying "There is no God but Allah."

Ironically, the tables were turned in the sixteenth century when the Spanish Christians regained their strengths and African and Arab influences lost ground. The Spanish explorers in Central America appealed to the Spanish crown for slaves to do the hard work of mining and digging. Africans and Arabs in Spain were given a similar choice: accept the Christian faith or be sent to the New World as slaves. Four thousand were shipped from Spain to Central America in 1503.

After its rise to power in Europe, the Christian Church practiced slavery. At one time the church was the largest dealer in slaves.

When comparing the enslavement of whites over blacks in terms of better or worse—history has shown that no slavery is better.

XIV

Kahina: Jewish, African and Defiant

For a time Queen Kahina of Numidia blocked the spread of Islam toward Carthage. She also checked its movement southward into Western Sudan. Her battle was a difficult one for several reasons. The Christian Church was growing very political. The Roman armies were becoming strong and worrisome in the Middle East and North Africa. Kahina saw these two events making the rise of Islam possible.

It was a mystery why Queen Kahina chose to fight the spread of Islam over that of Christianity. She was neither. She followed the Jewish faith. Yet her love for Africa was strong, almost overpowering. She did not want to see a foreign force changing the ways of the Africans. She used all of her power and her military skill to hold back the Arab tide.

General Kuseila of Mauritania was a relative of Queen Kahina. He began the first military resistance to the spread of Islam in North Africa. After he was defeated in 682, Queen Kahina became interested and angry. When he was killed six years later, Kahina rode into battle against the Arabs.

A skilled rider, a master with the sword and the commanding voice of a general, she outfought the Arabs. She drove them north into Tripolitania. Her attacks and counter attacks were so fierce and so well-directed that Arab governors had doubts about trying to conquer Africa after all.

The Arab high command took a second look at Kahina when top Arab General Hassan-ben-Numann had to retreat from Carthage. He had captured it in 698 but could not hold it. In 703 A.D., Kahina scored a clear victory over the enemy at Thamugas. Two years later in 705 A.D., she dug in at Thysdrus in an old Roman amphitheater. Her battle with Hassan took place at the foot of the Aures Mountains. This time she was beaten.

Nevertheless, Kahina fought on. The followers of the dead Kuseila helped her as she kept the Arabs off balance. In one time of desperation, when she was in danger, she ordered fertile farm lands destroyed to create a shortage of food and shelter for the invaders. This proved unwise. Research has shown that some of this destruction of valuable land can be seen today, 1,300 years later.

The longer the war proceeded, the more the Arab governors debated. Should they continue to fight the fierce and skillful queen? Should they forget the conquest? Yet the battles raged on with Kahina's emotional cry of Africa for the Africans. General Hassan stayed in the war. He dogged her tracks, both in defeat and victory. One new plan after another was devised to defeat her.

Finally in 705 she was wounded and died almost instantly. Later historians did her an injustice by calling her "The Joan of Arc of North Africa." Kahina lived a thousand years before Joan. The French martyr might have been called "The Kahina of France."

XV
Africans Saved the Byzantine

When the Byzantine Empire was created by transferring the capital of the Roman Empire to Constantinople, Africa became more important than ever in world trade. Her role in providing economic support to the empire—during the early days of the Middle Ages—was revealed only a half century ago. When historians realize to what extent ancient African trade is linked with the later support of the Byzantine Empire, they will view the African past with new respect.

Even before the seat of the Roman Empire was moved, Africa had joined with China, India and Persia in providing vital goods to Constantinople. This trade maintained the great Mediterranean city's economic and cultural leadership in the Mediterranean world. It was this basic economic assistance to the economy of Constantinople that enabled her to endure.

By 800 A.D., the circulation and distribution of gold as a medium of exchange had declined. Having only debased silver to pay for goods, the Byzantine Empire needed access to gold for economic stability. At different periods of its existence, Persia had used roadblocks on the Mediterranean to limit the supply of gold to the East. During another time after the Arabs had captured Egypt and seized control of the Red Sea, the empire was doomed to collapse. Even considering that these two damaging interruptions occurred within a one-hundred-year span, African gold shipments managed to get through to the Byzantine.

Earlier, during the sixth century, Nubian caravans and Abyssinian ships delivered needed commodities to the Byzantine. It was also long before the movement eastward that a vigorous trade from Central Africa found its way within range of Roman markets.

At one time, an Abyssinian king controlled the gold trade from his country. He hired 500 agents to search his country's interior. They bartered with salt and iron for precious golden nuggets the size of green peas. When the Byzantine traders bought these nuggets—which actually were less valuable than the Byzantine coins—they made enormous profits for the empire.

Trips to and from the Byzantine were often round about on purpose. Some of the shipments would start as far away as modern Kenya, even though, as an observer named Steven Runciman wrote, "This gold came mainly from Nubia to which the Romans had access." The observer might have added that Abyssinia to the northwest and other African lands were also suppliers. Several other colorful items were supplied to Constantinople by Abyssinia and the Somali Coast. They were ivory, ostrich feathers, spices, frankincense and myrrh.

Constantinople had various sources of ivory but the finest quality was shipped to her from East Africa. Even earlier, Roman historian Pliny had written: "Flavius Arrianas tells us that the African product was superior to that of Arabia."

There was also a generous market between the Romans and the Africans for tortoise shells, hides, wild animals and ebony. All of these were used for Roman dress in the fifth and sixth centuries.

These are significant facts that will overturn the negative remarks by some historians and give a new insight in helping to keep the Byzantine Empire stable. Africa contributed to the upcoming western civilization. This was a civilization about which some western historians have said Africa had absolutely no part.

XVI
Struggle of Early Black Christians

Before there was a Europe with its imposing cathedrals in France, Spain, Germany and Italy, before there was a London with its mighty Westminster Abbey, there were blacks in North Africa who held the struggling Christian Church together. While writers have emphasized Rome as the site of persecuted Christians, it was in North Africa where Roman armies killed and maimed the followers of the Church. Fanatics from other religions also burned the buildings and the homes of the faithful. Most important, black Carthage was the chief seat of the entire Christian movement.

Carthage was a black nation and a huge North African city. In the early Christian Church, the most zealous members were blacks. At one point during the struggle against persecution, black Saint Cyprian, one of the fathers of the early Church, called a conference of bishops. Eighty-seven bishops attended from Nubia, Mauretania, Ethiopia and Carthage—all black nations. Later in 411 A.D., Saint Augustine, who was another black father of the early Church, called a meeting of bishops from the same countries.

Carthage was in a natural position to assume control over the early Church. The church began in Africa and Carthage was second only to Rome as an educational center, having produced some of the greatest Roman writers and orators of the time: Saint Augustine, Saint Cyprian, Tertullian, Arnobius, Lactantius, Minicus Felix, Clement, Origen and Athanasius.

Roman emperors exerted awesome pressure on the Christians in efforts to exterminate them. In 242 A.D. Emperor Valerian sent soldiers. Their damage hurt the Church, but did not destroy it. Even earlier, the Black Emperor Septimius Severus had sent his legionnaires. Next to the worst of all was Emperor Decius. He randomly spilled the blood of Christian followers.

The modern world thinks that only in the arenas of Rome were

Christians fed to wild animals. It was in Carthage, too. They were shoved into arenas before lions and tigers.

In North Africa, the Christian Church movement was always in danger. Roman soldiers not only attacked the Church, they also refused to provide protection from the zealots of other faiths. Three black Carthaginian women were killed by fanatics from other faiths. They were Felicita, Nymphano and Perpetua.

The church suffered another powerful blow. Emperor Diocletian sent such military strength against the Christians that they felt the end had come. He declared that he wanted the Christian Church out of his empire. Again the most avid confessors and gifted defenders of the faith rallied. Their roots were too deep for Diocletian's armies to tear away. The Church survived.

Later the Christian Church was taken into Europe but before that happened it migrated into the rest of the Roman Empire by way of Africa. It is an irony that the great Cathedral of St. Louis in North Africa now stands on the same site in Carthage where Black Saint Cyprian challenged the government of Rome.

XVII

Abderrahman Saved African History

Blacks and historians throughout the world have Arab travellers to thank for preserving the history of African kingdoms. Without their fair reports on the African civilizations during the Middle Ages, there would be no resources that shed light upon this important period in Africa's past. The false name of the "dark continent" would still be with us.

There were several outstanding Arab travellers and writers whose works have shed light on Africa. They tied her African activities in with the rest of the intercourse among nations from 400 A.D. to the discovery of America and afterwards. One of the most outstanding of these writers was Abderrahman es Sadi, a Black scholar of Timbuktu. His book, *Tarik es Soudan*, is one of the most reliable references to be found on African kingdoms. Authors of the most informative books today use this text as their prime reference.

What distinguished *Tarik es Soudan* from other writings of its time is the author's extensive research. Abderrahman traced the great Kingdom of Songhay from its ancient days to the development of Ghana. The book describes Songhay's merger with Mali and the final greatness of the Songhay Empire. Special mention is also made of the days when Songhay was a small ancient kingdom with direct ties to the kingdoms of Egypt. For instance, a Pharaoh once sent to this small kingdom for a magician to outdo the miracles of the prophet Moses. It was at this time that the god of the people of Songhay was a fish. *Tarik es Soudan* says "The first king of Songhay was Dalliman and he came from Yemen."

Tarik es Soudan lists the names of the dynasties that ruled Songhay. There was Dio, the first dynasty. King dio Sobo had trouble with his enemies. Later came the better known Sunni dynasty of Sunni Ali. This soldier king expanded his kingdom. he ruled from 1464 until a year after Columbus touched the Americas. The last dynasty was that of Askia. Askia Mohammed, or Askia the Great, ruled one of the largest empires on earth. The Songhay empire was larger than all of Western Europe. The country extended from the Atlantic Ocean back to the Lake Chad region. *Tarik es Soudan* describes in great detail Songhay's system of education with its universities at Sankore and Timbuktu, the extensive agriculture, the sea and land trade, the art, the construction and how the government responsibilities were divided.

Tarik es Soudan extends its records beyond the fall of the Songhay Empire. The author describes the black people of Morocco and Massina. He also describes the Tauregs, the Mossi, and the Ouolofs whose descendants, the Woolofs, are found in Mexico today. Teachers and students alike have found Abderrahman's research of African kingdoms valuable. Scholars and objective historians have praised his *Tarik es Soudan* for providing a healthy balance to other historical writings.

The German explorer and writer Heinrich Barth, the English journalist-historian Lady Flora Lugard, and Felix Dubois all liked *Tarik es Souden*. Barth said the book was "...one of the most important additions that the present age has made to the mankind of history." Lady Lugard, who travelled and wrote extensively on Africa, judged the book an invaluable document for the light shed on the manners, the life, the politics and the literature of the continent. Felix Dubois was the most generous of all in this praise. He said Abderrahman's book was "the greatest work of all literature of the Sudan, produced in the final days of its twilight." He added that the book was a charming guide through the Sudan. "It reflects the life and mind of the Sudan of yesterday. It forms the favorite volume of the Negro as is known to the furthest extent of West Africa, from the shores of the Niger River to the border of Lake Chad."

For almost two centuries after it was written, the *Tarik es Soudan* was lost. Had it remained available, there is no way of knowing what other historians might have done with it or to it. Therefore, its absence may have been a blessing. As for now it offers proof that African kingdoms did exist, that they were civilized, productive, intelligent and well-organized; that they provided knowledge, scientific information and trade techniques to Europe and North Africa.

Most important Abderrahman es Sadi had the foresight to prepare a document which preserved the dignity of Africans throughout the world.

XVIII
Treasures of Ancient Nigeria

Arnold Toynbee was one of the many distinguished English scholars who degraded Africa. A world famous sociologist and economist, he wrote the Industrial Revolution in 1884. This book has been relied upon by economists. Since that time, Toynbee has been quoted throughout the world as having said that Africa contributed nothing to world civilization.

Among the scores of recent discoveries now disproving the negative claims of Toynbee and others, is the traveling exhibit entitled "Treasures of ancient Nigeria: Legacy of 2,000 years." Those alive today, who agree with Toynbee, may reverse their opinion, especially when they see ancient Nigerian art. World art critics have judged it to be "the greatest art created by mankind."

Some of these masterfully done pieces were created 500 years before Christ. The handiwork shows a superior intelligence and a facile adaptation to the environment in which the Nigerians lived.

When it is realized that the ancient Nigerians worked with bronze 2,500 years ago, no opinions which demean them are true. A comparison of the history of this period of high creativity with general history reveals that the Romans of that time were crude farmers with a nagging and worrisome relationship with the nearby Etruscans. Yet at this time, the Nigerians were creating magnificent figures of heads, people, animals, and jewelry in bronze, terracotta, ivory and stone. One hundred pieces of this revealing art are now on a world tour.

The immortal artist Picasso was significantly influenced by African art. This is admitted and taught in art classes everywhere. At first, some European art critics could not accept African art, "which said what it meant" rather than being elaborately descriptive. Some say African art broke all of the rules that modern artists have been taught in learning how to tell African art from European. But African art is realistic in form, classical in style, finished to perfection and definitely advanced in technological skill. Some of the cast and sculpted heads are compared with classical Greek work. The intricate and complex vases also have been compared with the finest examples of Chinese bronzes.

Without preaching against the negative critics of Africa in general and blacks in particular, the Nigerian art exhibit silently proclaims that Africans did contribute to world progress and civilization. They lived in a healthy, intellectual and progressive society. Their art lends dramatic support to the overlooked facts that ancient Nigerians were tradesmen, farmers, herdsmen, miners, scholars and healthy worshippers of their God. Societies best prove their level of civilization through their art. As such, through their art Nigerians have debunked all criticisms.

It was a momentous occasion in the Nigerian village of Nok, in 1943, when the 2,500-year-old terracotta sculptures were unearthed. If the exhibit called the *Treasures of Ancient Nigeria* serves only one purpose, it is to support the fact that Nigerian slaves brought to this country have practiced their heritage here...and that they were *somebody* before the discovery of America.

XIX
Early African Religions

The majority of blacks in America are Christian churchgoers. They adopted the religion of their slave masters and followed it with great fervor. In the African countries from which Black Americans came there still remain the roots of their ancient religion and their gods. Since Africa has been proved to be the birthplace of mankind, the need to understand how the African's religion developed has become basic to understanding the other religions that followed: Islam,

Africans made and played stringed instruments used in their worship.

Hare Krishna, Buddhism, Judaism and Christianity.

These recent religions all have strong similarities to the basic African religions of centuries ago. They include deep concern and reverence for ancestors, respect and concern for one another, harmony among all people, dependence on the wisdom of elders and a strong belief in the hereafter.

In African religion no man could possibly stand apart from his faith. His religion was his complete way of life. It was evident in his fishing, hunting, farming, mining, metalwork, animal training and moving from one place to another. its practices also involved justice, love, truth, right and wrong, and man's rights and responsibilities. Beliefs affirmed man's need for a healthy relationship with his environment.

The more complex the African's life became, the more his religion reflected it. It was shown in his art, his dancing, his music, his singing and his invention of musical instruments and related artifacts.

As nations and groups of Africans migrated to all parts of the world, they took their gods and religion with them. The early gods of East Africa took root in Europe, Asia, along the coast of the Red Sea, South America and the West Indies. Evidences of their worship have been left in the form of wall paintings in caves. Some of these predate ancient Ethiopia and Egypt, and provide further proof of their respect for magic, marriage, family and the valuable proverbs of elders.

Major African beliefs regarding the hereafter agree substantially with existing religions: *If one lives a clean and honorable life, following all of the tenents mentioned above, then he will receive his reward in a beauti-relaxed hereafter.* Africans held many ceremonies and festivals to illustrate their beliefs. They had holy places and religious objects—sacred hills, charms, marks and rivers. There were rain makers, medicine men, priests and ritual elders. Sometimes the king or the highest ruler was head of the religion.

In the African religions there was no preaching. Religion belonged to the people who believed they could live *only* within *their own* religious context. Their faith resulted in the deaths of hundreds of thousands who would not convert to Islam. The close-knit spiritual practices could be performed only by members of a family, a relative, or the people of an entire village or settlement.

People depended upon religion as needs arose. The African faith developed in this light, from pre-history through the Middle Ages. Factors beyond the African's control would change the course of his religion such as earthquakes, thunder storms, volcanoes, changes in seasons, epidemics, deserts and forests, diseases, birth and death. Religion and its practice were earthly and realistic.

Contrary to what historians, novelists and movie makers have told us, the African religion was not based on superstitions, ancestor worship or paganism. It was, and still is, a major religious system in its own right. In parts of Africa its influence still remains and so does its gods...

In Angola, the God is Kalunga
In Ghana, the God is Bore-Bore.
In Liberia, the God is Yala.
In Zimbabwe, the God is Unkulunkulu
In South Africa, the God is Mawri.
In Tanzania, the God is Enrai.

African religion had no sacred books. The invisible records were written in the hearts and the experiences of these prehistoric and ancient people.

XX
Endless Ethiopia

Black people kept one nation alive for 3,000 years before there was a Europe, even longer than any other nation in Asia or Africa. For 5,000 years Ethiopia has been foremost in world affairs. The Bible mentions her 49 times. Homer, a poet of classical Greece, made generous mention of Ethiopia in his *Illiad* and *The Odyssey*. Very few nations on earth did not have dealings with Ethiopia. The Hebrews called her "Cush" meaning "Black". Others called her Abyssinia. Still others referred to her as "Ethiopia." At one time in history Ethiopia and Egypt were *the* two world powers, similar to Russia and the United States today.

The uncertain way that some European historians tell of Ethiopia is confusing. Either through carelessness or on purpose, they play Ethiopia down while they make other nations look important. When Makeda, Queen of the Ethiopian Province of Sheba, visited King Solomon of Judah, that nation is described as a powerful, prosperous and huge nation. While Solomon appeared to be in the class of a world ruler, the facts were that Ethiopia was 2,500 years older than Judah and far wealthier.

When Makeda presented Solomon with gold and precious stones that were worth millions of today's dollars, her gift substantially raised the financial status of Judah. Ethiopia was also involved in extensive trade with the world by ship and by camel. Her vessels sailed the Red Sea and the Mediterranean Sea.

By embracing the Christian Church even before it was called "christian," Ethiopia assumed an early supportive role in the founding of the Church. Ethiopia had her own famous saints and her martyrs, who died to preserve the Church's early growth. For centuries Ethiopia was the bedrock of the faith, harboring and nourishing the persecuted and the condemned. Her temples and churches, many hewn from a single rock, are some of the finest and greatest in the world. Her priests, church organization and orderly worship were rec-

Makeda — The famous Queen of Sheba with an Ethiopian priest.

ognized by such distinguished historians as George Rawlinson and Sir Wallis Budge, both Englishmen.

Ethiopia has long been acknowledged the "Mother of Egypt." Scholars from the Byzantine claimed that Ethiopia had the first organized society on earth. She was the first nation to create laws, government and marriage. No other government west of the Orient played such a vital role in world history.

According to the Bible, one of the distinguished sons of Ethiopia was Nimrod, King of Babylon. He was called a "Mighty Hunter for the Lord.." The Scripture also extolls Ethiopia's greatness in Isaiah as "The land of rustling wings which is beyond the rivers of Ethiopia that sendeth ambassadors by sea." Even earlier in history, the nation's early influence was cited as a beginning source of the famous Nile River.

Meroe, a later capital of Ethiopia, was even larger than Memphis, in Egypt. Her great temple to the God Ammon was the largest in the Nile Valley. The walls of this magnificent structure were built 15 feet thick of cut stone. It was 30 feet high. Many temples like this one remain standing today throughout the Ethiopian kingdom.

Researchers have discovered ancient furnaces for smelting iron in Ethiopia, revealing that Ethiopians mastered the technical skills required for the process three centuries before Christ. During the 12th century, they were making the best quality of iron in the world. River and dock accommodations for loading iron to ship to other nations have also been found. One of Ethiopia's largest customers was Egypt.

Although European historians have not agreed upon what historical relationships existed between Ethiopia and Egypt...it is a fact that they coexisted for 5,000 years. Researchers digging into the earth have found evidence that for 150 years Egypt was dependent on Ethiopia. Egyptian records support the fact that the kings of two Egyptian dynasties were appointed by Ethiopian overlords. During different periods of history, Ethiopian armies came to the aid of Israel and Judah. Ethiopia fought as well, against Israel and Judah as enemies. Blacks also saved Jerusalem from capture and thereby saved the Jewish religion.

Hereen, an authority on antiquity and ancient peoples, had this to say: "When the educated Greeks scarcely know about Sicily and Italy, Ethiopia was celebrated in the verses of their poets. They spoke of them as a wondrous nation and the most just of men and the favorites of the Gods." It was Hereen who also observed that the records of Egyptian priests were full of accounts of Ethiopia.

Ethiopia once ruled most of Asia. According to the famous Greek historian Herodotus, Ethiopia was considered to cover most of Asia, Arabia, Egypt and Palestine. Thus the nations of inner Asia located on the Tigris and Euphrates Rivers have entwined their history with that of Ethiopia. No nation has lived on earth since the beginning of recorded time that did not know about or have to deal with this black nation.

XXI

The Last Empire Bows Out

Monomotapa was a great black empire in south and southeastern Africa. It included Zimbabwe, Mozambique and an area to the south stretching into Transvaal. It touched and used the Indian Ocean and the Zambesi and Limpopo Rivers. At its peak, the empire was said to have covered 250,000 square miles.

The German writer Herbert Wendt felt that the Egyptians founded the highly civilized and productive empire and that the Bantu-speaking blacks took it over later. These blacks were called Shona and migrated into the ancient civilization of Monomotapa. Wendt further claimed that these blacks worshipped the sun and the moon and that sisters married brothers—just as the Egyptians did. Some researchers, however, have seriously contradicted Wendt's claims. One of his most reliable opponents was British archaeologist Dr. Gertrude Caton-Thompson. She not only refuted his statements but said that all of the finds, including buildings and artifacts, were definitely African.

Today 4,000 ancient mines can be found stretching across the southern region of the old empire proving the Iron Age was a strong and supportive aspect of the civilization. Other data supports its high degree of sophistication. Gold, a prime commodity for export to other nations, was mined in an area that measured 600 miles by 700 miles. Although the people did not prize their farming as much as their iron, they cultivated unique farmlands on the sides of hills that were watered naturally by rains rolling down the mountains and hillsides. Full access to the Indian Ocean further enhanced the prosperity of their empire.

Some historians place the arrival of the Bantu in southern Africa between 1000 and 1200. The Bantu were the clever people who built the great walls at Zimbabwe.

Around 1499, the Portuguese ships rounded the southern tip of Africa and came upon Monomotapa. They saw the emperor who ruled over this extensive land. He traded gold and manufactured goods with the nations that used the Indian Ocean ports.

The Portuguese accounts of the emperor's palace are still with us. They described it as the most elegant of anything they had ever seen. Rafters, floors, window sills, doors and beams were all covered with shining gold. Candlesticks made of ivory were inlaid with gold. Plates and dishes were of the finest porcelain. As happened in numerous African countries where gold and silver were involved, the Arabs and Europeans came. The results of centuries of empire-building then began to go downhill.

Intricate and involved political maneuvers, tribal infighting and the skillful European manipulations of the land and peoples moved the empire farther and farther away from its former grandeur. Monomotapa died slowly, as the land changed from the hands of Africans to the hands of Europeans. The empire did not dissolve entirely, however, until a few years after the discovery of America.

Until three years ago, Monomotapa, or what was left of it, was comprised of apartheid South Africa and tumultuous Rhodesia. Since then, the latter has been reclaimed by blacks and is once again Zimbabwe.

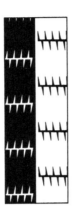

References and Suggested Reading

List of References For Blacks Before America

African History And Culture. School District of Philadelphia. African American Studies. William Green, Dir. 1980
Baker, George Phillip. *Hannibal* . New York. Dodd Meade. 1929
Boule, Marcellin. *Fossil Men*. New York. Dryden Press. 1957
Bovill, E. A. *The Golden Trade of The Moors*. 2nd ed. London. or Oxford University Press.
Bovill, E.W. *Caravan of the Old Sudan*. London. 1933
The Golden Trade of The Moors. London. 1933
Breasted, James. *A History of Egypt From The Earliest Times To The Persian Conquest*. London. Russell and Russell. 1905
Britt, L. W. *Makers of South Africa*. London. T. Nelson. 1944
Browder, Anthony T. *Nile Valley Contributions To Civilization*. SP 1992.
Brunson, James. *Black Jade: The African Presence in the Ancient East*. DeKalb, Il. KARA Publishing Co. 1985
Budge, Wallace Ernest. *The Egyptian Sudan: Its History and Its Monuments*. London. Paul French Tribner. 1907
Chu, Daniel and Elliott Skinner. *A Glorious Age in Africa*. New York. Doubleday. 1973
Cottrell, Leonard. *The Lost Pharoahs*. Westport, Conn. Greenwood Press.
Davidson, Basil. *The Lost Cities of Africa*. Boston. Little-Brown. 1959
——— *The African Genius*. Boston. Little-Brown. 1969
——— *History of West Africa to the Nineteenth Century*. New York. Doubleday. 1965
——— "African Kingdoms. " Morristown, NJ. *Times Inc*. 1966
——— *Africa in History: Themes and Outline*. New York: Collier Books. 1974
——— *The African Past*. Boston, Little-Brown Co. 1964
——— *The Lost Cities of Africa*. Boston. Little-Brown. 1959

DeGraft-Johnson, J.C. *African Glory*. Baltimore: Black Classic Press. (1954)

Delafosse, Maurice. *The Negroes of Africa*. Washington, D. C. Associated Publishers. 1931

Diop, Cheikh, Anta. *The African Origin of Civilization*. New York. Lawrence Hill and Co. 1974

——— *Civilization Or Barbarism*. Brooklyn, NY. Lawrence Hill Books. 1991

Dixon, Roland. *The Racial History of Man*. New York. Scribner and Sons. 1923

Dobbler, Lavinia and William Brown. *Great Rulers of the African Past*. New York. Doubleday. 1965

DuBois, W. E. B. *The Negro*. 1915

——— *The World and Africa*. New York. International Publishers. 1946

Dunn, John. *Cetewayo and The Three Generals*. Natal. Natal Printing and Publishing Co. 1886

Dunston, Alfred G. Jr. *The Black Man in the Old Testament and His World*. Philadelphia. Dorrance. 1974

Dupuy, Ernest and Trevor. *The Encyclopedia of Military History*. New York. Harper and Row. 1968

Drake, St. Claire. *Black Folk Here and There* (An essay in history and anthropology). Los Angeles: Center For Afro American Studies. 1987

Fagg, William. *Nigerian Images: The Splendor of African Sculpture*. New York. Praeger Pub. Co.

Fleming, Beatrice J. and M. J. Pride. *Distinguished Negroes Abroad*. Washington, D. C. The Associated Publishers. 1946

Gilbert, Charles-Picard. *Life and Death of Carthage*. New York. Tapinger. 1968

Githens, Thomas S. *Drug Plants of Africa*. University Museum, University of Pennsylvania Press. 1948

Githens, Thomas and Carroll E. Woods, Jr. *The Food Resources of Africa*. (African Handbooks #3). University of Pennsylvania Press. 1943

Hansberry, William Leo. *Pillars in Ethiopian History*. (From the

notebook of William Leo Hansberry. Vol. I, edited by Joseph E. Harris. Washington. Howard University Press.) 1977
"Hatshepsut" *New York Times*. January 27, 1932.
Hawkes, Jacquette. *Pharoahs of Ancient Egypt*. New York. American Heritage Col 1965.
Herodotus. *Histories of Herodotus* (Translated by George Rawlington.) New York. Tudor Pub. Co. 1928.
Herskovits, Mellville. *The Myth of the Negro Past*. New York. Harper and Brothers. 1941
Huggins, Willis. *An Introduction To African Civilization*. Avon House. 1937
Hyman, Mark. *Blacks Who Died For Jesus*. Nashville, TN. Dereck-Winston.
Idowu, Bqlaji E. *Oldumare: God in Yoruba Belief*. Canada. Longmans. 1962
Jackson, John G. *Introduction to African Civilization*. New York. University Books. 1970
Jones, Thomas M. "East African Influence Upon The Byzantine Empire. " *Journal of Negro History*. Vol. 43. No. 1, 1958
Johnson, E. Harper. *Piankhy The Great* . New York. 1962
Journal of African Civilization. Vol. 1, No. 1, New Brunswick, NJ. April 197 9.
King, N. Q. *Religions of Africa*. New York. Harper and Row. 1970
Kunjufu, Jawanza. *Lessons From History: A Celebration of Blackness*. Chicago. African American Images. 1987
Lamb, Harold. *Hannibal: One Man Against Rome*. New York. Doubleday. 1958
Little, Kenneth. "African Culture and World Intrusion. " *Journal of World History*. Vol. III, No. 4, 1957
Massey, Gerald. *Ancient Egypt: Light of the World*. Samuel Weiner.
Mbiti, John S. *Concepts of God in Africa*. New York. Praeger. 1970
McCray, Walter A. *The Black Presence in the Bible*. Chicago. Black Light Fellowship. 1990
Motley, Mary Pennick. *Africa: Its Empires, Nations and Peoples*. Detroit, MI. Wayne State University Press. 1969
Osei, Grabriel K. *The African, His Antecedents, His Genius and His*

Destiny. Hyde Park, NY. University Press. 1971

Peet, T. Eric. *Egypt and the Old Testament*. London: The African Publication Society. 1983

Philadelphia Tribune. Black History Month Edition. February 9, 1982.

Postel, William A. *The Mineral Resources of Africa*. (Africa Handbook No. 2. University of Pennsylvania Press, University Museum.) 1943

Rhoades, F. S. *Black Characters And References in the Holy Bible*. New York. Vantage Press. 1980

Rogers, J. A. *The World's Great Men of Color*. New York. Macmillan. 1942

Rogers, J. A. *Sex and Race*. New York. Helga Rogers. 1942

Sertima, Ivan Van. *They Came Before Columbus*. New York. Random House. 1976

Snowden, Frank M. Jr. *Blacks in Antiquity* . Cambridge. Belknap Press of Harvard University Press. 1970

Tietjens, Eunice. *The Romance of Antar*. New York. Coward-McCann. 1929

Tirharka. *Black Manhood*. Washington University Press of America. 1979

Wayne, Elizabeth. *The Pharoahs of Ancient Egypt*. New York. Random House. 1964

Weiner, Leo. *Africa and the Discovery of America*. Philadelphia. Innis and Sons. 1920

Wells, Evelyn. *Hatshepsut*. New York. Doubleday. 1969

Williams, Chancellor. *Destruction of a Black Civilization*. Chicago. Third World Press. 1974

——— *The Rebirth of African Civilization*. Washington, International Encyclopadea. 1965

Williams, Lorraine. *Africans and the Afro American Experience*. Washington, D. C. Howard University Press. 1974

Woodson, Carter G. *The African Background*, Outlines. Washington, D. C. Associated Publishers. 1936

——— *African Heroes and Heroines*. Washington, D. C. Associated Publishers, Inc. 1939

Wesley, Charles Harris. *Neglected Essays in American Negro History*. Washington, D. C. Association For The Study Of Negro Life And History. 1969

Windsor, Rudolph. *From Babylon to Timbuctu*. Jericho, NY. Exposition Press. 1969